TOWARD A GOOD CHRISTIAN DEATH

TOWARD A GOOD CHRISTIAN DEATH
Crucial Treatment Choices

———■———

Committee on Medical Ethics
Episcopal Diocese of Washington
Episcopal Church House
Mount Saint Alban
Washington, D.C. 20016

Committee members who developed this report:

Cynthia B. Cohen, Ph.D., J.D., Co-chair
The Reverend Dr. David Bird, Co-chair
Priscilla Cherouny, M. Div.
Frank W. Cornett, M.D., J.D.
Alex Hagerty
Patricia Lusk, M.P.H., R.N.C., N.H.L.
Virginia Oler, M.D.
Dorothy Rainey
The Reverend George Timberlake, Th.M.
The Reverend Dr. Joseph Trigg

MOREHOUSE PUBLISHING

Morehouse Publishing
P.O. Box 1321
Harrisburg, PA 17105

Morehouse Publishing is a division of the Morehouse Group.

Cover image: Corbis/Orion Press

Cover design by Annika Baumgardner

Library of Congress Cataloging-in-Publication Data

Toward a good christian death : crucial treatment choices / Committee
  on Medical Ethics, Episcopal Diocese of Washington ; committee
  members who developed this report, Cynthia B. Cohen ... [et al.].
        p.   cm.
  Includes bibliographical references.
  ISBN 0-8192-1800-6 (pbk. : alk.(paper)
    1. Terminally ill—Miscellanea. 2. Death—Religious aspects.
  3. Death—Moral and ethical aspects. 4. Christian ethics.
  5. Medical ethics.   I. Cohen, Cynthia B.   II. Episcopal Church.
  Diocese of Washington.   Committee on Medical Ethics
  R726.8.T67 1999
  174'.24—dc21   99-36306
                                                           CIP

Printed in the United States of America

Contents

Acknowledgments

We thank the following individuals, who have reviewed either portions of this book or the entire work, for their extremely helpful comments.

Gordon B. Avery, M.D., Emeritus Professor of Pediatrics, George Washington University School of Medicine, Washington, D.C.

Richard Beatty, B.L., Shaw, Pittman, Potts, and Trowbridge, Washington, D.C.

The Reverend Dr. Thomas E. Breidenthal, Professor of Moral Theology, General Theological Seminary, New York, New York

The Reverend Hugh E. Brown III, Assistant Rector, St. John's Church, Lafayette Square, Washington, D.C.

Courtney Campbell, Ph.D., Director, Program for Ethics, Science, and the Environment, Department of Philosophy, Oregon State University, Corvallis, Oregon

Holly Cohen Cooper, J.D., Bethesda, Maryland

Elizabeth L. Cuddeback, Washington, D.C.

The Reverend Randolph K. Dales, Rector, All Saints' Church, Wolfeboro, New Hampshire

The Reverend William J. Danaher, Jr., Associate Rector, Grace Church, New York, New York

Margaret A. Farley, Ph.D., Christian Ethics, Divinity School, Yale University, New Haven, Connecticut

The Reverend Sharline A. Fulton, Assistant to the Bishop of Pennsylvania and Adjunct Priest, St. Martin-in-the-Fields Church, Chestnut Hill, Pennsylvania

The Right Reverend Ronald H. Haines, Bishop of Washington, Washington D.C.

John Hausner, Erdenheim, Pennsylvania

The Reverend Dr. Jan C. Heller, Director, Center for Ethics in Health Care, Atlanta, Georgia

T. Patrick Hill, Research Scholar, The Park Ridge Center for the Study of Health, Faith, and Ethics, Chicago, Illinois

The Reverend Dr. Stephen Holmgren, Associate Professor of Ethics and Moral Theology, Nashotah House, Nashotah, Wisconsin

Samuel Holt, World Space, Washington, D.C.

Lynette H. Jacobs, Temple Hills, Maryland

Bruce Jennings, Executive Vice President, The Hastings Center, Garrison, New York

Stephen E. Lammers, Ph.D., Professor of the English Bible, Lafayette College, Easton, Pennsylvania

The Reverend Dr. Sandra M. Levy, Rector, St. Mark's Episcopal Church, Richmond, Virginia

Joanne Lynn, M.D., Director, Center to Improve the Care of the Dying, George Washington Medical Center, Washington, D.C.

Emily A. MacCormack, Washington, D.C.

Elizabeth Leibold McCloskey, M.T.S., Falls Church, Virginia

The Reverend Loren Mead, President Emeritus, The Alban Institute, Bethesda, Maryland

Margaret Mohrmann, M.D., Ph.D., Associate Professor of Pediatrics and Medical Education, University of Virginia Medical Center, Charlottesville, Virginia

The Reverend Dr. E. F. Michael Morgan, Rector, Church of the Good Shepherd, Athens, Ohio, and Chair, Committee on Health, Human Values and Ethics, Diocese of Southern Ohio

The Reverend Philip Paradine, Assistant Rector, Emmanuel Episcopal Church, Alexandria, Virginia

John H. Pickering, J.D., Wilmer, Cutler and Pickering, Washington, D.C.

The Reverend Dr. Charles Price, Emeritus Professor, Virginia Theological Seminary, Alexandria, Virginia

The Right Reverend Kenneth L. Price, Suffragan Bishop, Diocese of Southern Ohio, Columbus, Ohio

Judith Wilson Ross, Associate, Saint Joseph's Health Care System, Orange, California

Linda S. Samuel, M.S.W., Washington, D.C.

Margot Schultz, Kensington, Maryland

The Reverend Dr. David A. Scott, Professor of Theology and
  Ethics, Virginia Theological Seminary, Alexandria, Virginia

Timothy Sedgwick, Ph.D., Professor of Christian Ethics, Virginia Theological Seminary, Alexandria, Virginia

David H. Smith, Ph.D., Director, The Poynter Center for the
  Study of Ethics and American Institutions, Indiana University, Bloomington, Indiana

Martin L. Smith, S.T.D., Staff Bioethicist, Cleveland Clinic
  Foundation, Cleveland, Ohio

Andrew Stephen, *New Statesman,* Washington, D.C.

William Stubing, President, The Greenwall Foundation, New
  York, New York

Karen Roberts Turner, J.D., M.A., Montedonico, Hamilton, and
  Altman, Chevy Chase, Maryland.

Ann C. Urban, M.S.W., Swarthmore, Pennsylvania

The Very Reverend P. Linwood Urban, Emeritus Professor and
  Chair, Department of Religion, Swarthmore College,
  Swarthmore, Pennsylvania

Robert M. Veatch, Ph.D., Professor of Medical Ethics, Kennedy
  Institute of Ethics, Georgetown University, Washington,
  D.C.

The Reverend Dr. Francis Wade, Rector, St. Alban's Church,
  Washington, D.C.

The Very Reverend George L.W. Werner, Dean, Trinity Cathe-
  dral, Pittsburgh, Pennsylvania

The Reverend Pierre Whalon, Rector, St. Andrew's Episcopal
  Church and School, Fort Pierce, Florida

John S. Winder, Jr., J.D., Chevy Chase, Maryland

Of course, the Committee on Medical Ethics of the Diocese of
Washington is responsible for the final version of the material,
and our reviewers do not necessarily endorse all of the views
presented here.

We would also like to thank the Endowment for Mission and
Ministry of St. Paul's Episcopal Church, Indianapolis, Indiana,
for a generous grant enabling us to develop this book. ∎

I

Introduction:
Difficult Choices Near the End of Life

It is difficult for us to acknowledge that one day we will die. In earlier times, paintings sometimes showed ordinary men and women going about their daily business pursued by a skeleton tugging at their coat or tapping them on their shoulder—the figure of death. This skeleton was part of their everyday life, a reminder to them that death was inevitable. Today, in contrast, many of us go about our lives pretending that we will never die. No figure of death seems to stalk us.

Yet no matter how hard we may try to avoid thinking about it, there are moments that remind us that one day we will face death. The knowledge that we must die is background music playing faintly in the distance. It swells in volume and tempo when we or those close to us become seriously ill. At such times, death becomes more of a reality for us—especially if we must make decisions about whether to use powerful medical technologies to prolong our own lives or the lives of those dear to us.

Modern medicine has developed the capacity to keep us alive much longer than was possible in previous generations. Such measures as respirators, feeding tubes, and cardiopulmonary resuscitation (CPR) have improved the chances that those who are in fundamentally good health will survive an accident, heart attack, or stroke. But these remarkable medical technologies may only prolong the period of dying for those with multiple maladies who suffer such untoward events. Indeed, they may even make it difficult for us to figure out that someone is dying because they can keep people alive in the advanced stages of diseases that have no clearly defined terminal phase (such as chronic obstructive lung disease or Alzheimer's disease) for long periods of time. In such circumstances, we must decide whether to use all available life-sustaining treatments or not—knowing that our decision will affect when and how we and those we love will die. We are among the first generations to have to make these painful choices. And we should not gloss over the truth that, even when a medical intervention offers little hope of benefit, it is agonizingly difficult for us to forgo using it and allow the skeletal figure of death to enter.

The elderly father in multi-organ system failure on life-support in the intensive care unit, the middle-aged mother in a persistent vegetative state after a car accident, or the son with AIDS hospitalized for the third time with pneumocystis pneumonia—all these cases raise complex questions about whether to employ medical technology to prolong life. What treatment choices should we make for them and for ourselves when we are critically ill or suffering from a chronic condition that is leading to death? Should we always use the remarkable powers of medicine to fight against death? Or are there times when we should regretfully decline such treatment and request comfort care instead?

Questions abound. Are there circumstances or conditions under which we should choose not to be resuscitated? Will antibiotics for pneumonia prolong our life and allow us to gain some joy and feel some purpose to it—or will they only extend our dying? How well can our pain be managed? Has a relative, who cannot speak for herself at this point, made out an advance directive to give us a sense of what she would want done? If it is time to let our son go, how can we help him to have a good Christian death?

Jeremy Taylor, a seventeenth-century Anglican moralist, declared in *Holy Dying*, "It is a great arte to dye well." He emphasized that a good death involves not only hope and reconciliation at life's end, but a good Christian life. We should not prepare for death just before it arrives but over the course of an entire lifetime. Taylor recalled that the 1662 *Book of Common Prayer* declared in its Burial Service that "none of us liveth to himself and no man dieth to himself." He painted a picture of the person near death surrounded by family, friends, and ministers of the church.

When we envision the death we want today, our picture is often not that different. For many, a good death is a peaceful one in which we die easily and naturally, without discomfort, at home and surrounded by those we love. We share memories, become reconciled with one another, experience spiritual healing, and affirm our trust in the goodness and mercy of God. We close our accounts and finish our business in this life. A good Christian death, as the Anglican *Book of Common Prayer* declares, offers comfort, forgiveness, grace, strength, joy, and light.

Yet many of us fear that we will not have such a death. When we picture the death we want to avoid, we see medical technology extending our lives too long while we linger semiconscious in a sterile environment, perhaps in unrelieved pain and suffering. No family, friends, or ministers accompany us to the valley of the shadow of death. Abandoned, we fall into despair. The hope for faith, strength, mercy, and joy is absent from this vision of a bad death. It is a death we pray fervently to avoid.

In this book, developed by the Committee on Medical Ethics of the Episcopal Diocese of Washington (D.C.), we explore ways in which to make our picture of a good death become a reality. We elaborate on the contemporary art of dying in the face of new medical powers, setting aside the illusion that such powers will enable us to avoid death and achieve immortality. Our focus here is on decisions about the use of life-sustaining treatment for adults. We do not address difficult treatment choices that arise for children because these raise such special questions that we think they should be discussed separately. Although we consider many of the psychological, personal, and spiritual questions that can arise as death approaches, our main concern is with the ethical questions that we face when we must make decisions about the use of life-sustaining treatment. We discuss these from a Christian perspective from within the faith of a church based on Scripture, living within an ongoing tradition, committed to the use of reason, and encompassed in a sacramental structure of worship and spirituality.

The moral issues that come to light as we seek a good death in the face of today's medical capabilities are so new and so complex that it is difficult to find one approach to them on which all Christians agree. Yet there is a framework of central Christian moral teachings that sets limits to the differences that Christians may have. We set out this moral framework in general terms here and refer to it in various chapters in which we address specific questions that arise when making difficult treatment decisions. We recommend that readers who would like to go into these questions more fully also consult a companion book soon to be published by the End-of-Life Task Force of the General Convention of the Episcopal Church entitled *Faithful Living, Faithful Dying: Anglican Reflections on End-of-Life Care.*

Paul Ramsey, a prominent Christian ethicist, observed in *Who Speaks for the Church?* that whenever Christians come to a fork beyond which faith does not lead to a common mind, we ought to pursue each of the roads ahead to its end. We should provide arguments for following all roads, as well as cogent objections to this. In so doing, we may find that a common path emerges or, if not, that we have a better understanding of the significant landmarks that lie on each of the alternative roads. Such counsel has led our committee to try to avoid heated ideological debates as we have sought a common path and fresh insights into the views of others. When we have disagreed about issues, even in light of Christian teachings, we have sought a more complete understanding of the alternative moral roads available. Where possible, we have suggested ways in which these roads can meet. Our committee, which is composed of laypersons and clergy from within the Diocese of Washington, does not claim final authority about these crucial life-and-death treatment decisions.

We offer this book to those of you who face difficult choices about the use of today's medical capabilities—patients, family members, healthcare givers, clergy, pastoral counselors, and other interested persons. Although it is meant especially to assist those within the Anglican tradition, we believe it can also aid those of other religious traditions and those who adhere to none. We recognize the complexity of the situations in which you must make life-and-death decisions. Some of the uncertainty, pain, joy, and even tragedy such situations create will speak to you from the stories about difficult end-of-life choices that persons within or near our diocese have made that are included here. It is our hope that this book will encourage you to ponder in a prayerful way the roads you face as you make crucial treatment choices for yourselves and those you love, carefully considering the insights you derive from Scripture, the church's moral tradition, reason, and experience. ■

Discussion questions

1. Have you ever experienced the last stages of someone's life—family member or friend? Was the person or those close to the person faced earlier with having to decide whether it was "a time to die" (Ecclesiastes 3:1–2)? When he or she had to make that decision, was the person clearly "terminally ill" or was he or she in the advanced stages of a condition that had no clear terminal phase? What questions and concerns did the circumstances raise for you?

2. Have you ever thought about your own picture of "a good death"? In what manner would you would like to die, and what would you like to avoid at your death? What is it that you hope for and what is it you fear about dying? What makes these "end-of-life" questions especially important to you?

3. You may want to look up the following scriptural passages, which depict various death scenes: Deuteronomy 34:1–8; 1 Samuel 31:1–6; Luke 2:25–35; John 10:14–18; Acts 7:54–60. Do you think the dying process is "good" or "bad" in each of these scenes? Why?

2

The Anglican Moral Vision and Approach to Death

As we struggle to make crucial treatment choices that may lead to death for ourselves or those we love, we can draw upon the moral wisdom found in Christian thought, particularly the Anglican tradition. Our committee believes that values important to the Anglican tradition will resonate both with readers who share this tradition and with those who do not. Thus, we provide a brief overview of that tradition here.

a. What is the Anglican Communion?

The Anglican Communion is a worldwide Christian fellowship of churches overseen by bishops whose historical roots can be traced through the Church of England to the church of the New Testament. The various branches of the Communion, while independent and autonomous, are theologically and morally interdependent. Anglicans have typically laid great emphasis on the individual Christian's responsibility to achieve an informed conscience on moral questions. For this and other reasons, this tradition has maintained that the fundamental role of the church is not to tell people what to decide at key points in their lives, but to acquaint them with the moral principles and theological presuppositions that can guide their choices. More importantly, as a community of faith, the church provides a context of mutual accountability and shared wisdom. Individuals are not left alone to cope in making decisions but can share in the support of the community of faith.

b. Are there central Anglican beliefs, values, and ethical approaches that we can bring to end-of-life questions?

The faith of the Anglican Communion is grounded in Scripture, tradition, and reason and is nourished in a sacramental structure of worship. Anglicans, following the early theologian Richard Hooker, regard the Bible as God's word addressed to human reason. It provides witness to the events that lie at the heart of Christian faith and an interpretation of how a life based on that faith is lived. Anglicans believe that to view the Bible as a rule book is to overlook its capacity to awaken our reflection on God's purposes, as well as to betray its character as witness to God's relation to humankind and all creation. Nevertheless, Anglicans find throughout the Bible fundamental moral principles.

Tradition offers the accumulated and developing wisdom of the church. It amounts to a living process of discernment. Thus, when Anglicans appeal to tradition, it is not to say, "We've always done it that way," but to affirm that the church as the communion of saints exists over time. It is to indicate that Anglicans value tradition's wisdom as it responds to the biblical message in ways in which the Holy Spirit has guided it (John 16:13).

In this discernment, Anglicans call on human beings to use the full powers of our God-given reason. Anselm, an eleventh-century archbishop of Canterbury, wrote of faith seeking understanding. Like him, modern Anglicans see reason as an aid to faithful Christian belief and conduct. Reason, as Anglicans use the term, includes not simply intellectual analysis, but reflection on human feeling and experience. Anglicans therefore take seriously the way in which Christians still sense the voice or presence of God.

The primary embodiment of Anglican faith, aside from Scripture, is *The Book of Common Prayer*. The Prayer Book not only includes such statements of the church's teaching as the Creeds and the Catechism, but sets forth in its liturgies—from Baptism through Christian Burial—a comprehensive expression of what it means to be a Christian. When members of the Anglican Communion join with consenting minds in the worship of God set out in *The Book of Common Prayer*, we implicitly accept this understanding of the Christian life as our own. To do so is the primary expectation of the church for its members. Within this understanding of the Christian life, shaped by common worship and other sources mentioned earlier, Anglicans reckon with the moral complexities we all face.

Anglican moralists have embraced many traditional Christian moral principles and distinctions. Yet there is no single method by which Anglicans move from these principles and from the three major sources of moral authority—Scripture, reason, and tradition—to resolve moral questions in specific cases. Thus, deeply faithful members of the church have, at times, reached conflicting conclusions about specific questions because they have moved in different ways from principles to their application to issues. Indeed, the church has changed its position over time on important moral issues, such as slavery and divorce, as it has reworked the way in which it applies moral principles and its three major moral resources. Joseph Butler, an eighteenth-century Anglican moralist, observed that human nature and the circumstances in which we find ourselves are complex. Therefore, morality cannot be reduced to a single abstract formula, but must reckon with life in all of its concreteness and multiplicity.

Throughout its history, Anglicanism has embraced a moral vision displaying several distinctive features. These include:

- *A conviction that a moral order founded on God's wisdom pervades creation.* We can understand elements of this order and perceive God's purposes through the gifts of reason and grace. Anglicanism recognizes that our individual powers of moral reasoning are flawed and that at times we ignore this moral order and choose sinfully. Yet it also recognizes that God as Redeemer moves within the church community and within us, calling us back to the moral life.

- *A belief that it is essential to our relation to God to live a moral life, for in God, "we live and move and have our being"* (Acts 17:28). Indeed, by virtue of the Incarnation of God in Jesus Christ, we share the divine life, for, as Richard Hooker, an early Anglican theologian, declared in *Of the Laws of Ecclesiastical Polity*, God has "deified our nature, though not by turning it into himself, yet by making it his own inseparable habitation." The fullness of our human nature therefore requires that we develop our moral character and live in ways consonant with it, taking as our lodestar God's purposes for us.

• *A recognition that the moral life is not narrowly focused on the attitudes, desires, and intentions of individuals, but that it has a social dimension rooted in our communion in the body of Christ.* We are formed within our community and are called by God to recognize our relatedness to one another. This requires taking seriously the values of family, church, and community that draw us together.

• *A commitment to the values of love and justice, based on the beliefs that creation is good and that each person, as a creature made in the image of God, has unique worth.* That worth is a property we have as humans, regardless of any specific features we may possess as individuals, such as intelligence or beauty. Thus, we are each called to love one another and seek a just social order in which the dignity and worth of each person is recognized.

Given the openness of this basic moral vision, and the varying ways in which persons move from principles and resources to their application to issues, it is not surprising to find that different Anglicans and different branches of Anglicanism sometimes express divergent views on ethical issues. Anglican moral theologian Timothy Sedgwick makes this observation:

> Differences in moral judgments are not simply or narrowly matters of right and wrong. Rather, differences in judgment reflect differences in understandings that can be articulated, respected, and debated. . . . Christian ethics and moral theology provide the basis for critical reflection that informs moral judgments and promotes respect for those who may differ. ("Introduction," *The Crisis in Moral Teaching in the Episcopal Church*, Harrisburg, Pa.: Morehouse, 1992, p. 9.)

The Anglican tradition has a commitment to respect the differing views and positions that faithful people might reach on difficult moral issues.

This basic Anglican moral vision will guide us as we discuss moral, theological, and personal issues that arise at the end of life. Many of these are so new that they have not yet been given significant consideration within the Anglican and the wider religious community. The call to reason characteristic of the Anglican tradition and its belief—based on its view of the creation and the Incarnation—that wisdom is diffused throughout the world have historically led it to enter into dialogue with moralists of other religious traditions and secular ethicists. Therefore, as we grapple with the novel questions raised by our ability to apply our growing medical powers to persons at the end of life, we will also consider moral insights derived from other Christian traditions, other religions, and secular resources.

c. Is there an Anglican view of death and dying?

Anglicans neither minimize death's finality nor deny the grief and pain that normally accompany it. Anglicans perform funerals with a closed coffin and throw earth, that is, real soil, on the coffin in their interment service. Their funeral service does not discourage mourning and grief, but offers consolation and love to all who cast their grief on God. This is because the Anglican understanding of death and dying is grounded in Christian beliefs about the Incarnation, by which we mean God's becoming fully human in Jesus Christ, and about Jesus' resurrection from the dead.

A popular Anglican Christmas carol, "Once in Royal David's City," sings of a Christ who both "shareth in our gladness" and "feeleth for our sadness." This expresses our belief that God is manifest in the fullness of humanity. In his full humanity, in his living and his dying, Jesus reveals and reconciles us to God. Christians believe that by Christ's free acceptance of death, in obedience to the Father and for our sake, God has broken the power of death to claim the last word over our lives. When Jesus accepted death as part of his vocation to obey God and serve humanity, he transformed death into an opening up to the divine presence.

The Christian church, therefore, teaches its members to enter death in Christ—that is, to look upon their dying as a journey with Christ through death into the life of God. Death, while still retaining its dreadful and enigmatic powers, becomes, through faith, an opening up to the divine presence. Thus, Anglicans do not view death as an enemy outside of them capable of destroying all meaning in their lives. Rather, Anglicans believe that death, while still a terrible reality, is an enemy God has taken into his own life, through Christ, and overcome in him. Therefore, Anglicans believe we can move through death and resurrection into God's life.

Anglican prayer books, therefore, paint the picture of a good Christian death as one in which the dying person patterns himself or herself on Christ. In concrete practical terms, this means certain specific things. In *The Book of Common Prayer*, for instance, Anglicans ask God to sanctify the sickness of the person being prayed for, "that the sense of his weakness may add strength to his faith and seriousness to his repentance; and grant that he may live with you in everlasting life; through Jesus Christ our Lord. Amen" (p. 460). An earlier version of the Prayer Book advises that the dying person is to be in charity with the world, seeking forgiveness and forgiving others, reconciling and restoring relationships ("The Visitation of the Sick" in the 1552 *Book of Common Prayer*). There are practical requirements of the dying person in this older Prayer Book as well. He or she is to put all affairs in order, thoughtfully disposing of wealth and making out a will. In short, Christians are to prepare for death by living a faithful life, knowing that God actively wills our restoration to God and to each other. ∎

d. Discussion questions

1. How and when have you used the three main resources that the Anglican tradition uses to make decisions about end-of-life questions? Since many of these difficult questions have only come to light in the past fifty years, how can these resources, which appeared earlier, assist us in answering them?

2. You may find it helpful to look over pages 491–492 or page 496 of the Burial Rite in *The Book of Common Prayer*. What beliefs about life and death do you find embodied in this service? How might the approach that Christians take to death and dying

differ from that of those who are not Christian? How might it be similar?

3. Is it possible for Christians to share core beliefs about creation and death, and yet to reach different specific moral conclusions about end-of-life treatment? You will find that Romans 14:1–12 assists you in responding. What does this passage from Scripture suggest about how Christians are to reach mutual understanding about the difficult moral issues that arise at the end of life?

3

Choice, Responsibility, and Crucial Treatment Options

How do Anglicans answer the question, "Who should decide about the use of life-sustaining treatment?" You will remember that the Anglican Communion regards each person with respect because each of us was created in the image of God. This implies that human beings, as creatures reflecting God, are responsible for their actions. God, in the creation story, makes the first human couple responsible for the stewardship of creation and for keeping the command not to eat of the fruit of the tree of good and evil. God does not allow the man to avoid responsibility by placing it on the woman or the woman by placing it on the snake. This is an affirmation that human beings are called to engage in responsible moral choices. Therefore, the answer to the question, "Who should decide about the use of life-sustaining treatment?" is that we each should, as responsible persons living in community with one another and with God.

As we think over what we ought to do when we face terribly difficult choices about the use of life-sustaining treatment, we seek as Christians to do what God wants us to do. To this end, we use our capacity to reason as we look for guidance from Scripture as understood in the Christian tradition. We also take into consideration other religious and secular sources that throw light on our situation. Moreover, we call on the Christian community for insights and advice, consulting with our family, ministers, and friends.

a. Can we, as Christians, make whatever choices we want about the use of treatments near the end of life, or are there moral limits to our choices?

Secular ethicists, persons who have studied difficult questions about what we ought to do from the point of view of philosophers, often appeal to the concept of autonomy or self-determination to support the view that we ought to make our own treatment decisions. *Autonomy* literally means "being a law to oneself." Some of these ethicists seem to say that the principle of autonomy entails that each of us can choose or refuse any treatment we wish for any reason whatsoever. They tend to answer the question, "Who should decide about whether I should receive life-sustaining treatment?" with "I should."

Although the Anglican moral tradition also holds that we each have a responsibility to make informed decisions about our own care, it maintains that self-determination does not tell the whole story. We are people created, redeemed, and sustained by God. Thus, we view our freedom in the context of our covenant relationship with God. Ours is not an arbitrary and capricious freedom to do whatever we want, but the freedom to choose in ways that are rooted in God's actions and causes. Because we trust in the goodness of God, we are assured that freely choosing to serve God's purposes ultimately works toward our good. That is why we say that ours is a God "whose service is perfect freedom" (*Book of Common Prayer*, p. 57).

Moreover, our bodies and souls are God's, not ours. Paul reminds us that "you are not your own. For you were bought with a price; therefore glorify God in your body" (1 Corinthians 6:19–20). Thus, when deciding whether or not to use treatment that will sustain our bodies near the end of life, we are called not to displace God in our decision. We are to take account of significant moral values as we make such choices. These are set out in Section 4. Before we proceed to that section, however, we must first consider some important questions about decision-making procedures that we may face when we make crucial treatment choices.

b. Who can help us as we make crucial treatment decisions?

We need not shoulder our responsibility for making difficult life-and-death treatment decisions alone. We can call upon the Christian community for advice and support so that we do not feel overwhelmed. Our professional caregivers, ministers, family, and friends can each help us in different ways to think through what is at issue and what kind of medical treatment we want to receive.

i. Professional caregivers

Our doctors, nurses, and other caregivers are responsible for providing us with accurate and understandable information about our diagnosis, our prognosis, and the range of treatments available. We need to ask our physicians what a particular treatment involves, its likely outcomes, its side effects, and how it would help meet our treatment goals. Those of us with a serious cancer condition, for instance, need to know whether a particular treatment gives genuine hope of recovery or only a brief extension of life in considerable pain. Our nurses, who provide much end-of-life care, also will often provide us with meaningful information and insights so that we can understand matters more clearly. If we find that we are receiving somewhat different answers from different professional caregivers, we should ask to know which healthcare professional has final responsibility for our care and then request that he or she resolve these differences.

ii. Priests and other ministers

It is likely that our own priest, a hospital chaplain, or another pastoral counselor can help us when we are faced with difficult end-of-life choices. Such religious advisors are experienced in grappling with questions about the meaning of life and death and have been intimately involved in decisions people make about the use of life-sustaining treatment. Their training in Christian theology, ethics, spirituality, and pastoral care prepares them to help us make medical and moral choices in light of our common beliefs. As we wrestle with our deepest concerns and fears, they can offer us support, comfort, and prayers.

We may want a priest or pastoral counselor to sit through an especially difficult time with us, sharing our uncertainty, drawing out our questions, giving voice to our pain. Religious advisors cannot make the final choices for us, but they can help us to view our situation in light of the purposes of our loving and merciful God.

iii. Family and friends

Of course, our family and close friends are especially important to us at this time, not only because they can provide us with love and support, but also because they can help us explore the treatment avenues open to us. They can assist us in weighing our options and perhaps suggest alternate roads we may not have considered. It is extremely important to talk with those who are close to us at this time, for they can confirm our wishes to professional caregivers in the future should we be unable to do so. Indeed, at times we may need a family member to advocate for us long before we come close to death because disease and its effects hamper our energy, our ability to focus on "the big picture," and our capacity to make decisions.

c. Who can make treatment decisions for us when we cannot?

If we cannot make our own treatment decisions because our mental processes have been impaired by illness, someone who knows us well should make those decisions for us. Those who have written advance directives (see Section 3. e. below on advance directives) may have already used a durable power of attorney for health care to appoint someone to be what is known as a "surrogate" decision maker. If so, that person has the authority to direct our medical care at some later time if we cannot do so for ourselves.

If we have not made out advance directives, our family will usually be asked to speak for us when we cannot do so ourselves. Family members are often called upon informally to do this by doctors and nurses because they are assumed to know us well and to have a sense of what we would want. When close friends who clearly care about us are present through our critical illness, professional caregivers may seek their perception of the sort of treatment we would prefer. It is unusual for healthcare professionals to go to court to have a decision maker appointed for a person who has lost decision-making capacity, but this sometimes occurs.

Some states have passed laws that specify who should act as our surrogate and make medical decisions for us if we have not made out an advance directive. In those states, these laws tend to list decision makers in the following order of priority:

1. Our court-appointed guardian, if there is one
2. Our wife or husband
3. Any adult son or daughter
4. Either of our parents
5. Any adult brother or sister
6. Any adult grandchild
7. Our close friend
8. The guardian of our estate

Doctors and administrators of healthcare institutions in these states must go down the list until they find a person or persons available. If there is more than one person in the class, such as several adult children, all of them—or in some states, the majority of them—will be the decision makers.

When highly controversial decisions must be made, however, healthcare institutions may be reluctant to allow family members to make them. In the famous 1976 case, *In the Matter of Karen Quinlan*, Karen's father was not allowed the authority by the institution involved to be the decision maker for his daughter, who was in a "persistent vegetative state." (See Appendix A.) The New Jersey Supreme Court, however, gave him that authority and he, after talking with his wife and priest, decided to remove the respirator from Karen. Most states have followed suit and allowed families to make such decisions—but there are exceptions.

Thus, in the 1990 case, *Cruzan v. Director, Missouri Department of Health*, the law in the state of Missouri did not allow the parents of a young woman in a persistent vegetative state to make the decision concerning the use of life-sustaining treatment for her. Instead, state law required that the decision had to be guided by the wishes that the patient herself had expressed in a "clear and convincing" way—either verbally or in writing—when she was competent. Nancy Cruzan's wishes were not known when the case was first brought and therefore Missouri was unwilling to allow her parents to carry out their decision to end the use of artificial nutrition and hydration. The United States Supreme Court upheld this state law. It was only after state authorities received "clear and convincing" evidence of Nancy's prior wishes (which they had not had earlier) that they allowed life-sustaining treatment to be withdrawn from her at her parents' request. In the 1998 case of Hugh Finn in Virginia, family members disagreed about whether to remove artificial nutrition and hydration from a man who had been in a persistent vegetative state for three years. His wife was finally allowed to make the decision for him.

The lesson of these legal cases is that if we give those close to us clear expressions, verbally and in writing, of our wishes about the use of life-sustaining treatment when we are near death, these can be a great help to professional caregivers and judges.

d. On what basis should our surrogate choose for us?

If we have given some clear indications of our views about the use of life-sustaining treatment to our surrogate, he or she should be able to make decisions for us in light of our values and preferences. Having conversations with our surrogate and writing a "living will" can help ensure that our wishes will be respected when we are near the end of life.

Surrogates are to follow our explicit instructions. If we have given none, they are to use what is known in law as the "substituted judgment" standard, meaning that they should make the decision in the way that we would have made it. They are to substitute our wishes and values for theirs and then decide in the way that we would have decided.

Surrogates whom we have never told what sort of treatment we would want when we are near the end of life are to select or to refuse treatment on the basis of what would further our well-being. They are to decide this on the basis of what most reasonable persons would choose in these circumstances, which is known as the "best interests" standard in the law. This standard can create problems, however, because it can be difficult to know what most reasonable people would decide in certain circumstances. This difficulty provides additional reason for us to talk with our surrogate while we are still competent about the sort of treatment we do and do not wish to receive near the end of life.

e. What are advance directives?

Should we fall ill or have an accident and become unable to speak for ourselves, others will have to decide what sort of treatment to give us. Two sorts of documents, known as "advance directives," are available to assist those deciding for us in such circumstances. One lets others know what we want done at this time, and the other names someone who knows us well and whom we trust to make decisions for us.

The first sort of advance directive is known as a "living will." This is a document in which we indicate what sort of treatments we do and do not want should we become terminally ill or permanently comatose and unable to communicate. It does not appoint someone to make decisions for us. Instead, it provides a statement from us about the kind of care we want when we are clearly dying. In this directive, we can give our professional caregivers, family, and friends a sense of our basic values and religious and moral beliefs, indicating whether we would want no aggressive treatment in the sort of circumstance into which we have fallen or would want a great deal of it. We can also state in our "living will" whether we would want to have specific treatments, such as respirators and antibiotics, when we are terminally ill or permanently comatose.

All fifty states and the District of Columbia have laws that honor "living wills" and that provide guidelines for their preparation and use. These laws, however, vary from state to state. Some limit the medical conditions under which a "living will" takes effect, honoring it only when a person is clearly terminally ill—by which they usually mean the person has six months or less to live. Although it is important to obtain the proper legal forms for our own states, many states explicitly allow the use of documents that do not follow the standardized wording written into their laws.

Some of us may need to make a treatment decision in circumstances in which our "living will" does not apply. For instance, we may have a condition that does not have a clear terminal phase, such as Alzheimer's disease, and therefore may not be viewed as literally "terminally ill," yet our condition has put us on a downhill course that is leading to our death. By executing the second sort of advance directive outlined above, a durable power of attorney for health care, we can ensure that our surrogate makes treatment decisions for us in these circumstances if we are unable to choose for ourselves. Thus, the durable power of attorney for health care is especially useful if we are in the advanced stages of a condition that has not been labeled a "terminal illness."

In a durable power of attorney for health care, we appoint someone as our surrogate to make all medical decisions for us when we no longer can do so. A durable power of attorney differs from a regular power of attorney in that it takes effect when we lose decision-making capacity and become incompetent. A regular power of attorney, in contrast, no longer works when we lose decision-making capacity. The durable power of attorney for health care gives our surrogate almost all the rights we had when we were competent to make our own medical decisions. We can include directions to our surrogate decision maker about the kind of treatment we want and do not want in circumstances in which the "living will" does not apply. This might be the case, for example, if we are in advanced dementia and we no longer recognize those dear to us but are not terminally ill. Most states have laws that explicitly recognize durable powers of attorney for health care in situations where we cannot speak for ourselves.

The General Convention of the Episcopal Church supports the use of advance directives by patients and urges doctors and other healthcare professionals to recognize them. In 1992, the Seventieth General Convention declared in a resolution that

> Advance written directives (so-called "living wills," "declarations concerning medical treatment" and "durable powers of attorney setting forth medical declarations") that make [known]

a person's wishes concerning the continuation or withholding or removing of life-sustaining systems should be encouraged, and this Church's members are encouraged to execute such advance written directives during good health and competence and that the execution of such advance written directives constitute loving and moral acts. (See Appendix C. 2.)

If we have developed advance directives, we should make sure that everyone who needs a copy of them, such as our doctor and our surrogate, has one. We should also see to it that any hospital or nursing home that we enter receives a copy and writes into our records that we have an advance directive. If we enter a hospital or nursing home in a state other than our home state, we should see whether our directives apply there. If they don't, it would be wise to make out new ones that conform to the requirements of that state.

For further information about the use of advance directives, see the booklet, *Before You Need Them: Advance Directives for Health Care, Living Wills and Durable Powers of Attorney*, written by the Committee on Medical Ethics of the Diocese of Washington and available from Forward Movement Publications at (800) 543-1813. To obtain "living will" and durable power of attorney for healthcare forms authorized in your state, contact Choice in Dying at (800) 989-9455.

f. Need we do more than make out written advance directives to let others know our wishes about the use of life-sustaining treatment?

While it can be very helpful to our physicians, family, and friends to have these written advance directives, it is also extremely important that we talk with them about our treatment preferences near the end of life. We can start a discussion about our concerns about our care near the end of life with our doctor at the time that we give him or her a copy of our advance directives. Many physicians welcome these talks and ask thoughtful questions that help them to learn what we want done if we are critically or terminally ill with no reasonable hope of recovery.

Conversations we have about our advance directives when we get together with our families can help them to understand how to implement our advance directives. It is not easy to start these conversations. None of us wants to talk about our own dying. But it is important to do so, not only so that we receive the sort of treatment we want, but also so that we can ease the burden of decision making that our family and friends would otherwise face. They will find it difficult to make decisions for us when we are near the end of life knowing that our death may follow. Our guidance can be a gift to those we love that they will value increasingly as they care for us as we approach death.

g. Can we or our surrogate demand that we receive certain treatments?

Physicians are morally and legally required to honor the refusal of treatment by a competent patient or a surrogate. However, there is a long-standing medical tradition that discourages doctors from providing treatments that they believe will not benefit their patients. Many follow in the tradition of writers in the ancient school of Hippocrates who advised physicians "to refuse to treat those who are overmastered by their diseases, realizing that in such cases medicine is powerless." Today, the American Medical Association declares in its Code of Ethics that "physicians are not ethically obligated to deliver care that, in their best professional judgment, will not have a reasonable chance of benefiting their patients." Thus, when doctors believe that treatment would be futile, their professional association states that they need not provide it, even though patients demand it. However, as of this writing, every court case with a published opinion rules that physicians must deliver care requested, even if they object.

Deciding when treatment is futile is a highly controversial matter. Some argue that treatment is futile when it will not preserve the heartbeat and breathing (i.e., is "physiologically futile"). In this view, only when treatment is highly unlikely to keep the patient's body alive—as when there is little chance that resuscitation would start the patient's breathing in the last stages of a disease—would it be futile to provide it. Others maintain, however, that the definition of futility should be broadened to mean that treatment would be futile when in ninety-seven out of one hundred tries it would not keep the patient alive or would leave him or her either in a state of permanent unconsciousness or in need of intensive care for the remainder of his or her life. Those holding this view add that treatment also should be judged futile when it would leave a patient with a quality of life that falls below a threshold that doctors consider minimal. The treatment of many more conditions would be considered futile on this second view—persistent vegetative state, respirator dependency, or intermediate stages of Alzheimer's disease. This second view of the meaning of futility is controversial, however, because it allows doctors to make "quality of life" judgments of futility in situations when patients might well make different judgments. Thus, it opens the door to disagreements between patients, families, and doctors about when treatment should be stopped.

Should we or our surrogate request treatment that a physician considers futile, we need to talk with our physician about his or her reasons for judging that is would be futile. We need to learn about the treatment's effectiveness in clinical studies and what its side effects are. If, after discussion, we still wish to have the requested treatment and our physician still refuses to provide it, we can ask to have the matter reviewed by another physician or discussed by an ethics committee within the healthcare institution. (See Section 3. i. below on ethics committees). If the disagreement is not resolved by these means, we may have to go to the board of the institution or even to the courts.

h. What if disagreements arise about the sort of treatment we should be given?

In some situations, we (or our surrogate or family) may differ with professional caregivers about the sort of treatment that we should receive. In others, members of our family may be divided among themselves. The following story, seen through the eyes of one of the family, illustrates how differences may arise within a family. Here they were minor and were resolved within a family whose members clearly loved and respected each other. This story presents one way in which to resolve differences.

> My father-in-law suffered unremitting pain for the last two
> years of his life. Despite all manner of tests, doctors in his small

town did not detect inoperable lung cancer until two weeks before he died.

Although Dad was told when his cancer was discovered that he had six to eighteen months to live, my husband, his son, flew to his home immediately upon receiving the news. He wanted to give his parents some support as they came to terms with this diagnosis. I urged him to talk openly with his parents about the benefits of hospice for Dad when he neared the end. Four days after my husband's arrival, Dad was in such intense pain that he was taken by ambulance to the local hospital. He was admitted for treatment of pneumonia.

Mom (my mother-in-law) and my husband were stunned by the news of pneumonia, but even more stunned when they saw Dad in his hospital room. He was hooked up to all kinds of monitors, catheters, and breathing tubes. His hands were restrained because he kept trying to pull out the breathing tube. Despite the fact that Dad had long ago stated he did not want extreme measures taken to keep him alive when death was near, it seemed that his wishes were not being fulfilled.

When my husband called me and told me about Dad, I decided to join him. He picked me up at the airport and told me that during the night Dad had passed the nurse a note on which he had written, "I want to die." Mom, my husband, his sister, and I drove to the hospital immediately, and, after a while my husband asked his father in several different ways, "Do you want to die?" "Are you ready?" Dad shook his head indicating yes each time the question was asked.

We were only allowed to see Dad for ten minutes every two hours, so we went home to call his doctor and inquire whether he considered Dad a candidate for hospice. He said he was. However, Mom resisted. She felt that she wasn't ready to let Dad go. My husband, sister-in-law, and I believed that we should try to convince Mom to have Dad admitted to hospice care; we felt that we couldn't let him continue to suffer. We talked this over with Mom and finally she agreed that the process of moving Dad from the hospital to the hospice should begin.

Four hours later, Dad was in the hospice. The hospice doctor explained that they would ease Dad's pain with morphine and Valium and would begin to wean him from the assisted-breathing apparatus the next morning. However, Dad was never relieved of that apparatus and never conscious enough to communicate with us after he was admitted to hospice. He died less than twenty-four hours later, one week after his son's arrival in Texas.

I am convinced that Dad should have gone straight from home to hospice, rather than have been admitted to the hospital. Better yet, he might have had hospice care in his own home. Had his doctor encouraged this, he might have had a chance to say goodbye to us.

At one point, however, during the day that they started the attempt to wean him, I began reading aloud "Ministration at the Time of Death" and the anthems and psalms from "The Burial of the Dead: Rite One," both of which are found in *The Book of Common Prayer.* My husband concluded our prayers by reading aloud the collect for the burial of an adult. Immediately, Dad's breathing became less labored. For several minutes, we thought he might have died because the machinery's infusions of oxygen were suddenly spaced very far apart. Our doctor son-in-law had told us that hearing is the last sense to go, and I am convinced that Dad heard our prayers at that time. The memory of our last prayers with Dad gives me a sense of peace.

Judith M. McDaniel

The family involved in this decision came to an agreement fairly quickly after an initial period in which they were inclined to make different treatment choices. The fact that the author of this story was not only a close family member but also an Episcopal priest undoubtedly helped them to come together and make the difficult decision to let "Dad" go. We, too, may find it helpful to ask a priest or pastoral counselor to assist us when we are not sure about what should be done and need to have someone with fresh insights on the scene.

As noted above in our discussion of futility, if serious conflict arises between caregivers and families or within families and it cannot be resolved, a hospital ethics committee can be consulted for an advisory opinion. (See Section 3. i. below on ethics committees.) Sometimes these committees can bring together those who disagree and help them sort out their differences. Should disagreement continue, a court decision can be sought. This expensive and time-consuming legal alternative, however, is a difficult one for families to pursue.

i. What are institutional ethics committees and what do they do?

Most healthcare institutions have established ethics committees that can provide a procedure for resolving conflicts in particular patient care situations that raise ethical questions. Healthcare professionals or patients and their families may ask for an ethics committee opinion about a wide variety of questions. For instance, they may ask a committee for advice about whether to proceed with treatment that, though it may prolong a person's life, would do so at the cost of great pain and suffering. They may raise the question of whether a doctor must provide treatment that a family demands but that the doctor believes is futile. They may review a decision to move a patient into an intensive care unit when that patient indicated while on a regular nursing floor that he did not want to receive life-sustaining treatment. Ethics committees can provide a well-rounded perspective on such issues for those concerned.

Members of ethics committees can include individuals from many different backgrounds: doctors (both senior and junior), nurses, medical ethicists, social workers, clergy, administrators, patient representatives, community representatives, lawyers, and dieticians. In some institutions, an individual ethics consultant, a small team, or a clergy person may serve in place of an institutional ethics committee.

An ethics committee should strive for a respectful process that is open to all relevant "voices" and views, and also to relevant moral values. The main goal of such committees is to support and protect the well-being and autonomy of patients. Most ethics committees sincerely attempt to do this. However, a few ethics committees with a preponderance of members whose professional work is closely tied to the interests of the institution have been viewed by some as advocating more for their institutions than for patients. They have focused on how to protect the institution from lawsuits or extra costs. This can be a matter of concern for patients who are considering consulting with such a committee. To get a better sense of whether it would be wise to consult an ethics committee, we can ask to see a printed brochure about the committee, if there is one, that tells us how it works. We can also meet with an ethics committee representative and ask some of the following questions:

- Who is on the committee? How are they chosen?
- What sorts of ethical issues does the committee review?
- What procedures does the committee follow?
- What input do patients or surrogates have into the committee's discussions and conclusions? Do patients have a right to be present? To consent to a discussion of their situation by the committee?
- How is a final decision usually reached?
- Are the committee's conclusions only advisory or are they binding?
- If an ethics consultant, not a committee, provides counsel when ethical questions arise, is that person required to report to a responsible authority?

If we gain a sense that the committee has a well-conceived procedure for addressing ethical questions and is focused on the interests and needs of patients, then it could be wise for us to ask to have a formal consultation with it if we have an ethical question about our treatment. ■

j. Discussion questions

1. How do you respond to the question, "Whose choice is it?" What values or beliefs of yours lead you to give this answer? Are there passages of Scripture or prayers that are important to you as you think about what you want done when you are near the end of life? Consider, for instance, Genesis 1:27.

2. We can provide a great gift to our families by deciding whether or not we want to have life-sustaining treatment used when we are close to death, and then indicating our preferences in a "living will." What would your family want to know about your preferences at that time? How do you hope they will respond to the instructions you provide for them?

3. Perhaps you have been asked to serve as a surrogate for a close friend with no immediate family and are named as such in his or her durable power of attorney for health care. What questions do you want your friend to answer about his or her preferences about treatment near the end of life? Do you think you will find it difficult or easy to be a surrogate? Why?

4. Have you appointed a surrogate to make decisions for you should you become unable to make decisions for yourself? If so, have you told others in your family and friends close to you about your appointment of this person as your surrogate? If you haven't, do you plan to do so?

5. The story related in the section above about a moderate family disagreement may resonate with you. Have you had a similar experience or do you know someone who has? Can you put yourself into the role of each of those involved? How do you respond to their feelings and their decisions?

4

The Morality of Stopping or Withholding Life-Sustaining Treatment

Most of us would agree that we would like to ease the burden of decision making that we or others face when crucial decisions must be made for us about the use of life-sustaining treatment. We would like to be prepared, and would like to prepare those we love, to address challenging questions that may arise about what treatment to use at different stages of a terminal condition or a chronic illness leading to death. But how do we begin to sort through our own views? Are there any concepts in Christian or secular moral thinking that can help us work through the complicated circumstances we might find at the end of life and help us make our choices? How should we begin to think about these questions? A very significant notion that has been developed within the Christian tradition can help us: the distinction between proportionately beneficial (ordinary) treatment and disproportionately burdensome (extraordinary) treatment.

a. What do we mean by proportionately beneficial (ordinary) treatment and disproportionately burdensome (extraordinary) treatment?

Many of us have heard of "ordinary" and "extraordinary" treatment from reading newspapers and watching television stories about patients who are critically ill and near death. Christian and secular moral thinkers have used these concepts to distinguish treatments that are morally required from those that are morally optional. Some have found the terms *ordinary* and *extraordinary* confusing, however, and today, moral theologians and ethicists instead tend to use the (much longer!) terms *proportionately beneficial* or *disproportionately burdensome* instead.

Proportionately beneficial (or ordinary) treatment is treatment that offers more benefits than burdens. It is morally required for us to use because, in a Christian ethic, we are called to care for our bodies—the temples of God—as part of our whole selves. Disproportionately burdensome (extraordinary) treatment is treatment that offers us more burdens than benefits. It is treatment that we are not morally obliged to have. As Christians, we are not morally required to accept any and all burdens that may be in the offing in order to remain alive. (See Section 4. b. immediately below on whether we must do everything possible to keep a person alive.)

What counts as a benefit when we are deciding whether treatment would, on balance, be beneficial or burdensome? There are certain things most people would count as benefits—removing a diseased organ, halting the growth of cancer, living long enough to say goodbye to those we love. What about burdens? Again, there are some things that most people would agree count as burdens—receiving treatment that has no reasonable chance of benefiting us, experiencing extreme pain and suffering, having radical or disfiguring surgery, going to a medical center at a great distance, or having treatment that is extremely expensive.

However, what count as benefits and burdens, for Christians, is not just a matter of common agreement or even of personal preference. It is also a matter of Christian ethics. Thus, living long enough to be reconciled with those from whom we have been estranged would count as a benefit in a Christian ethic because it fulfills Christ's call to us to love one another (John 13:34). Receiving an expensive experimental drug of doubtful effectiveness whose use would bankrupt our family would count as a burden in a Christian ethic, as it runs counter to that same call. The weight of the burden of our treatment on our family also enters into consideration for Christians.

We must balance all these sorts of benefits and burdens in light of our Christian ethic and then make a decision about whether to proceed with treatment. This involves weighing many factors in our specific situation—a situation that may be riddled with uncertainties. We must ask such questions as:

- Does the treatment have a reasonable chance of success as far as doctors can tell?
- What degree of invasiveness and pain will it create for me?
- What could be its outcome? In what sort of condition would it leave me?
- How would its use affect my family and others?
- What is its financial cost?

If, after careful consideration of the answers in light of our values as Christians and the uncertainties we face, we conclude that the benefits of a treatment are greater than its burdens, that treatment is proportionately beneficial and to be used. But if its burdens are greater than its benefits, that treatment is disproportionately burdensome and need not be used. Such decisions can be very difficult to make because often there are no clear answers to some of our questions. We must make the best choices that we can under these circumstances.

For instance, we may find that the use of a respirator to assist us to breathe over a long period of time is physically burdensome and does not offer the benefit of reversing our course toward death. We may realize that we do not have an obligation to try to remain alive as long as it is humanly possible to keep us alive (see section 4. b. below) and we may believe that we have given the respirator a good try. We may therefore regretfully conclude that we should withdraw the respirator and ask that our physician take care that this will be done in a comfortable way.

In another sort of situation, we may decide that even though we have a serious chronic condition that will ultimately lead to our death (such as chronic obstructive lung disease) the benefits of major surgery outweigh its burdens. This might be because the surgery would extend our life for about a year—a time during which we could have a good life. Therefore, we may elect to undergo this procedure.

Each of us may make different decisions about when treatment is beneficial or burdensome, even though we share similar

Christian values. Joan, for example, may believe that chemotherapy to slow down the growth of a cancerous tumor would be disproportionately burdensome because it would make her feel significantly more wretched and lethargic. She may also believe that there are no significant acts, such as making amends to a close friend or attending a child's marriage, that she ought to perform in the extra time that chemotherapy would give her. Thus, Joan may decide that the burdens of chemotherapy outweigh its benefits in her case, and she may decide against it.

Sam may come to a different conclusion, even though he is in a similar situation. He may willingly submit both to chemotherapy and to risky surgery to remove a similar tumor, even though the cancer has spread. For Sam, chemotherapy and surgery would offer the benefit of possibly living a little longer to see a grandchild graduate from college and to set his personal affairs and relationships in order. Such benefits outweigh the burdens of this treatment for Sam, and treatment would be proportionately beneficial in his case. Although Sam and Joan cherish the same values and ethical standards, their individual circumstances differ and so they reach different conclusions about whether or not to receive further treatment.

It is important to realize that treatment is not considered disproportionately burdensome because it is sophisticated or exotic. Treatments that are simple to provide, such as antibiotics, can become disproportionately burdensome when they would provide us with no overriding benefit. It is not how unusual a treatment is that makes it disproportionately burdensome, but whether its burdens outweigh its benefits.

Finally, it is also wise to recognize that medical treatment is of a whole person who has a history and life goals—not of a collection of organs and body parts existing at this moment. That is, when we make a decision about whether to use a certain treatment we must consider our overall goals as persons and Christians, not just how to attempt to fix things that are malfunctioning at this minute. In the case of Karen Quinlan cited above, who was in a persistent vegetative state, the goal of treatment was to return her to a conscious state of life, not to keep her lungs functioning. When her parents accepted that she would never regain consciousness, they concluded that keeping her lungs functioning by mechanical means offered Karen no overriding benefit and, after consulting with their priest, removed the respirator.

b. Must we do everything possible to stay alive out of respect for the sanctity of human life?

Some hold that the goal of treatment for all patients should be to keep us alive for as long as possible. "As long as there is life, there is hope," they declare. This view, which is known by theologians and ethicists as *vitalism*, holds that life itself is the greatest possible value and that it should be sustained at all costs.

Christian moralists have seldom adopted this position. Indeed, in his book, *Church Dogmatics*, theologian Karl Barth cautioned against making life another God. He and others recognize that if life were our highest value, it would be wrong for saints and martyrs willingly to give up their lives for their faith. Indeed, it would be wrong for us to drive in cars or to take plane trips, for we know that human lives can be lost on highways and in the air. While human life is extremely valuable because it has a sanctity given it by God, it is not our highest value. As the example of saints and martyrs tells us, values such as love of God and one another can be morally more weighty than the value of life. Thus, when we are near death and treatment would be either useless or disproportionately burdensome, we can let our life go.

Thomas Wood observes in *A Dictionary of Christian Ethics*, "It has been claimed that, until death occurs, it is always one's duty to continue using to the full every available life-sustaining procedure. But, when one considers all the highly sophisticated systems and techniques of modern medicine, it is frightening to envisage the possible consequences of a strict adherence to such a rule." He maintains that we must take into account other important values in addition to life and weigh them in the balance according to Christian beliefs and insights. The 1992 General Convention of the Episcopal Church recognized this, stating that "there is no moral obligation to prolong the act of dying by extraordinary means and at all costs." (See Appendix C. 2.) We are not morally required to make every possible effort to stay alive by means of medical treatment.

c. Is it wrong to stop life-sustaining treatment once it has been started?

At times, it is useful to try a life-sustaining treatment for a trial period to see whether it will be effective. Each of us has our own unique way of responding to a disease, and a disease may progress in different ways in different people; the trial period gives physicians time in which to assess whether treatment will be effective for us as individuals. This is known as a "time-limited trial" of treatment. For instance, a patient who appears to be in end-stage congestive heart failure (or that patient's surrogate) might agree with the treating physician to a two-day trial of monitoring and aggressive treatment. If, at the end of this time, she does not appear to have improved, but is losing ground, efforts to reverse her condition would stop and she would receive comfort care. If she showed signs of improving, however, she would continue to be treated. Here is what one physician says about such time-limited trials:

> I find it helpful to tell patients and families that I cannot know the patient's reserve and the behavior of the disease well enough to stop treatment at just the right time. Generally, I tell them that the best I can do is to overtreat each patient a little, since that is often what I need to do to understand the body's reserves. I promise, however, that I will make every effort to keep these trials brief. Once it is clear that they are not warranted, I will avoid repeating treatment that has failed because the patient's dwindling reserves limit the capacity to rebound back to baseline function. Patients and families are usually reassured by the overall approach and are generous in forgiving our uncertainties. Confident that a good care plan can be crafted, patient and family fears about ambiguity and uncertainty are generally relieved, not heightened, by honesty. (Joanne Lynn, "An 88-Year-Old Woman Facing the End of Life," *Journal of the American Medical Association*, 1997, 277[20]:1633–1640 at 1636.)

Some physicians and patients, however, feel that while it is right not to start life-sustaining treatment that may prove useless, it is wrong to stop such treatment once it has begun. They notice that there is an emotional difference between stopping useless treatment and not starting it in the first place. Yet many Christian and non-Christian moral thinkers would say that although there is an emotional difference, there is no moral difference between them. Let us explain this.

It is never easy to withdraw life-sustaining treatment once it has been started. When it is first begun, there is some hope, no matter how slight, that it will help a patient to improve. Sometimes this hope is realistic. At other times it is not. What has been called the "technological imperative" can push us to use it and all other available medical technology, as T.S. Eliot wrote in another context,

> Not for the good that it will do
> But that nothing might be left undone
> on the margin of the impossible.
>
> —T.S. Eliot
> (*The Family Reunion*, Part 1, Section 1)

If this treatment does not turn the patient's condition around within a reasonable period of time, hope for recovery fades and those involved are bound to feel terribly disappointed. Some may want to overcome their disappointment by denying that the life-sustaining treatment is not working. They may ask the doctors to "do everything possible." It is the emotional difficulty of stopping life-sustaining treatment at such times that leads some to say that once it has begun it is not morally acceptable to stop it.

However, if it is morally right not to start treatment that will be ineffective, it is also morally right to stop such treatment when it is discovered that it does not work or no longer works. This is why most Christian moralists say that there is no moral difference between withholding and withdrawing treatment. Should we realize that life-sustaining treatment has not been effective, it is morally appropriate to stop it. While anyone who has had to make this decision knows how agonizingly difficult it is, we can be sustained by the knowledge that it is the right thing to do.

d. Will God work a miracle and cure those of us who are critically ill or dying if we pray hard enough?

Many faithful Christians turn to the hope of a miraculous healing when all hope of a recovery by other means is lost. Should we, too, do this?

The Bible shows that God acts in the world. In the Old Testament, for example, we find the "wondrous" parting of the Red Sea at the Exodus. In the New Testament, we read of the "mighty works" of Jesus, many of which were acts of healing. In John's Gospel, miracles are often described as "signs" of the Kingdom of God. The miracles recorded in Scripture are occurrences that faith recognizes as acts of God. It is not the strength of our faith that causes God's miraculous actions; rather, by faith we recognize and receive God's miracles.

Whether God has freely decided to operate within the laws of nature, to change them on behalf of individual persons, or to give us a different experience of the course of nature is a matter on which Christians are divided. Even so, they unite in believing that God actively seeks the health of each person. Consequently, whether we should expect miracles in those medical situations when scientifically all other hope is lost will be a matter of individual belief and conscience.

Many of us have heard of people diagnosed with a terminal illness who unexpectedly have been restored to a full life and diagnosed as free from disease. In some cases, their deep faith in God appears to be a significant part of the healing process. Such happy instances make it even more difficult to deal with the many cases in which physical healing does not occur in persons of deep faith. People who are not healed after much prayer sometimes ask, "What is wrong with my faith?" or "Why am I unworthy of salvation and God's healing?" In their anguish, they may believe that God has abandoned them.

In some cases, such questions are raised because we think of prayer as only a petition to change what we believe is the mind of God or else to alter the course of events. We may forget that there is another dimension to prayer: listening to God and waiting upon God's presence. Thus, the Episcopal Church's *Book of Common Prayer* includes numerous prayers in which we ask God to enlighten us, strengthen us, purify us, and direct us. *The Book of Common Prayer*, for example, includes the following prayer for a sick person to use:

> This is another day, O Lord. I know not what it will bring forth, but make me ready, Lord, for whatever it may be. If I am to stand up, help me to stand bravely. If I am to sit still, help me to sit quietly. If I am to lie low, help me to do it patiently. And if I am to do nothing, let me do it gallantly. Make these words more than words, and give me the spirit of Jesus. Amen. (p. 461)

Our most heartfelt prayers are not always answered in the manner we have asked. Prayers for healing of those in a terminal condition, almost without exception, are for physical healing in this life. The Christian believes, however, that dying can be a genuine answer to prayers for healing. It may not be the way in which we had hoped our prayers for healing would be answered, but it is healing because it is the means to a fuller life with God. It is beyond our finite limitations of knowledge and insight to determine who may or may not be healed physically by prayer, anointing, and services of "faith healing." Yet we must recall that it is unwise to put all of our hope in those cases in which the miraculous intervention of God has restored people to physical wholeness—not because it doesn't happen, but because it is so unusual. We can place ourselves firmly in the hands of God, secure in the faith that our life will be transformed (no matter what the outcome of the disease process), raised up, and accepted with the "sound of trumpets and in the twinkling of an eye" at the table of the Good Shepherd. ∎

e. Discussion questions

1. Which view of the value of life is closer to your own, the vitalist position that we must sustain life at all cost or the view that we can let life go in some circumstances? How would you support your position if challenged?

2. Have you ever had an occasion when you had to decide whether life-sustaining treatment would be more burdensome

than beneficial? If so, what were the circumstances? For whom did you have to make this decision? What did you decide? Have there been times since then when you have worried about it? If so, what have you done to reassure yourself about that decision?

3. Can you recall scenes in the Scriptures in which people went to great trouble to try to keep alive those who were dying? What about scenes in the Scriptures in which people were allowed to die without any attempt to stop the death? How do these scriptural passages affect your view of what we should do today about the use of life-sustaining treatment?

5

Decisions about Using Specific Life-Sustaining Treatments

Many different kinds of treatments can be used to sustain our lives, including cardiopulmonary resuscitation (CPR), respirators, blood transfusions, endotracheal tubes, antibiotics, dialysis, surgery, and artificial nutrition (food) and hydration (fluids). Continuing to use such treatments can allow a patient to have a good Christian death. But at times questions arise about whether the use of such treatments should be ended. Each of them raises distinctive questions of its own, so it is important to think through what the benefits and burdens of using the particular treatment at issue are. In this book, we cannot possibly cover all those treatments that are available to sustain life. Therefore, in this section we focus on a few to give us a sense of what sorts of ethical questions withdrawing or withholding each of these specific treatments raises. This, in turn, will give us some insight into how we might begin to address questions that arise about other life-sustaining treatments.

a. Under what circumstances might we consider refusing life-sustaining treatments?

Before we discuss specific life-sustaining treatments, we will want to think in general about under what circumstances we might consider refusing or stopping them. Although it is hard to conceive of all the circumstances in which we might view life-sustaining treatment useless or burdensome, patients have made morally appropriate decisions to refuse or stop life-sustaining treatment in a number of circumstances, including the following:

- when an illness is highly likely to take a downhill course toward death, regardless of treatment

- when available treatments would increase the probability of a painful and protracted dying, even though they might extend life for a while

- when the only effective treatments available for a possibly fatal condition are likely to cause extreme pain and suffering

- when treatment, if successful, would create or sustain extended unconsciousness

- when treatment is available only at a distant medical center and getting there would require separation from family and/or great expense

In these sorts of situations, many patients or their surrogates have decided that the use of life-sustaining treatment would be disproportionately burdensome and have decided to ask for comfort care instead. (See Section 6 below on relieving pain and suffering.)

To get a better sense of when treatment can be beneficial or burdensome in light of overall patient goals, we will now look at the use of three specific life-sustaining treatments: cardiopulmonary resuscitation (CPR), artificial nutrition and hydration (provision of food and fluids by technological means), and antibiotics.

b. Accepting or refusing cardiopulmonary resuscitation

i. What is cardiopulmonary resuscitation and how is it done?

Cardiopulmonary resuscitation (CPR) is a procedure that can be used to try to restore breathing and the heartbeat in a person when these have been unexpectedly stopped because of some sort of injury. The person performing CPR breathes into the mouth (often using a bag or mask), filling the person's lungs with air, and then applies pressure to the chest with his or her hands to expel it. This procedure was originally developed for healthy people who had been in an accident, such as a near drowning or severe electrical shock, that had caused their breathing and heartbeat to "arrest," or stop. The use of CPR saves the lives of many such people each year.

In recent years, the use of CPR, in combination with other resuscitative techniques, has been extended to hospitals and nursing homes. In the hospital, if a patient's heart stops, a "code" is called, and a team responds. The team uses not only CPR, but injections of medications, electrical shocks to the heart, a tube down the throat to keep the airway clear, and mechanical respirators, among other techniques, to attempt resuscitation. In a nursing home, if a resident's heart stops, CPR will be started and the staff will call the rescue squad or fire department. In many states, the paramedics from these agencies will continue CPR and do everything possible to keep a person alive while they transport him or her by ambulance to the hospital emergency room.

ii. What are some of the distinctive benefits and burdens of using CPR?

Although CPR was originally designed for people who could be restored to their previous state of health, it gradually came to be used for patients in a wide variety of chronic conditions who were on a downhill course toward death. Eventually, anyone who suffered an arrest had a "code" called, no matter how poor his or her condition. This has led many to weigh its distinctive benefits and burdens carefully.

CPR can bring a major benefit: survival in the condition that we were in before we arrested or in a condition fairly close to it. Whether there is a reasonable chance that it would do this in our case depends on our medical condition and prognosis.

Yet CPR can also create burdens. During the procedure, our ribs might be cracked or a lung punctured because of the force that must be applied. If too long a period of time has elapsed between the arrest of our breathing and heartbeat and the start of CPR, we may suffer brain damage due to lack of oxygen. Further, those of us in declining health with several serious medical problems who have an arrest have little likelihood of surviving to leave the medical institution. Studies suggest that most patients over age seventy with several serious medical problems who receive CPR in the hospital do not remain alive long enough to go home again. Those who are resuscitated and leave the hospital have only a slim chance of long-term survival and their medical condition is likely to be worse than before the arrest occurred. Few nursing home residents who are given CPR and taken to the hospital live to return to the nursing home. Those who do survive with their mental capacities intact tend to reject the idea of any further CPR attempts, should they arrest in the future, because they have found the procedure too burdensome to endure again. Consequently, caregivers no longer assume that CPR is always to be used for each patient.

iii. How can we reach a decision about whether to use CPR when we are terminally ill or in the advanced stages of a disease?

Mindful that we are not obliged to try to sustain life by every medical measure available to those near the end of life, we will want to consider whether the use of CPR would bring a balance of benefits to us. We can ask whether CPR could restore us to our previous condition or whether it might leave us in very poor condition. What is our overall prognosis or outlook? Would resuscitation change that prognosis for the better?

Because of the drawbacks of using CPR, many people in poor health with multiple medical problems have requested that this procedure not be done should their breathing and heartbeat stop. However, others who are in a similar condition have decided that the benefits of CPR are worth its burdens and they choose it. Making this decision requires that we reflect carefully on what we know about our medical situation, on our social situation, and on our values. If we decide that CPR would be too burdensome, we can instruct our physician to write a "Do Not Resuscitate" (DNR) order (also known as a "No Code" order) into our medical record. This tells other members of the staff of the hospital or nursing home that they are not to resuscitate us should we stop breathing or have a cardiac arrest. If we are at home and have had a DNR order written into our records, it is advisable to tell others not to call the local rescue squad should we experience an arrest. We can also wear a bracelet indicating this so that should a rescue squad be called when our breathing and heartbeat have stopped, despite our previously expressed decision, members of the squad will know that we are not to be resuscitated.

Here is how one family decided about whether to use CPR for a member who could no longer make his own decisions and who had a serious medical problem.

Josh K. was a retired, highly successful businessman who took a warm interest in his family, as did they in him. In his later years, he developed a serious heart problem and severe dementia. His wife, Sarah, whose own health was declining, found that she could no longer care for him at home. She arranged to have him placed in a nursing home nearby that could provide Josh with excellent care.

On admission, Sarah was asked if Josh was a "No Code." This meant that the staff wanted to know whether to resuscitate Josh should he suffer a heart attack. Sarah had not thought about it before and decided at that moment that he should be resuscitated. She therefore declined to have him listed as a "No Code." Afterward, their daughter, Barbara, questioned whether this was an appropriate decision for Josh. She suggested to Sarah that they convene a family meeting to discuss it, and her mother agreed. Sarah said she would consult with Josh's doctor to get his medical opinion about the condition in which resuscitation could leave Josh, and George, their son, said he would talk with their priest about it. Each of them said they would find out as much as they could about CPR before the family meeting.

Sarah brought several articles from medical journals that Josh's doctor had given her about CPR in elderly persons with major medical problems. These indicated that people in Josh's condition, if resuscitated, were highly unlikely to return to their previous state, but might, instead, become even more debilitated. Moreover, the procedure itself might be very traumatic for Josh, who would not understand why it was being done. Their doctor, Sarah told them, had recommended against CPR for Josh for these very reasons.

George reported that their priest suggested they discern what benefits and burdens CPR could provide for Josh, and then weigh these against each other to gain a sense of what would be best for him. Christians are not morally obligated to keep a person alive for as long as humanly possible, she had indicated, and she had recommended that they prayerfully consider whether Josh was reaching the "time to die" mentioned in Ecclesiastes. She promised to talk with them further after she had visited Josh in the nursing home.

After a few weeks had passed and the family had held several more discussions with their doctor and their priest, they reluctantly decided that it was best for Josh not to receive CPR. Sarah then had a "No Code" order entered into Josh's records at the nursing home. He lived for another year until he had a heart attack in his sleep and died peacefully.

Sara Aguilar

The decision whether to be resuscitated or to resuscitate someone whom we care for deeply is an emotionally wrenching one for patients and their families. However, it need not be made in isolation from those close to us and from the church. We can talk it over with our family and friends, with our priest and our physician, before coming to a final decision.

c. Accepting or refusing artificial nutrition (food) and hydration (fluids)

i. What do we mean by "artificial nutrition and hydration"?

When we can no longer take food or liquids by mouth, we can receive liquid nutritional supplements through a feeding tube. This is known as artificial nutrition and hydration. "Nutrition" refers to preparations that are a substitute for solid foods and "hydration" to substitutes for water and liquids. The food supplements used in providing artificial nutrition today look like a milkshake and contain calories, vitamins, and minerals that can sustain those taking them.

Two different types of feeding tubes can be used for this purpose: a nasogastric tube, a soft plastic tube that is run through the nose, down the esophagus, and into the stomach; and the gastrostomy tube, which is inserted surgically through the skin and stomach wall into the stomach. Intravenous (IV) lines may also be used for nutritional supplementation that is not meant to be long-term. With an IV line, liquid flows through a catheter attached to a needle in the arm or leg.

ii. What are some of the distinctive benefits and burdens of artificial nutrition and hydration?

Feeding tubes can offer great benefits to many patients. Some individuals need them only for a short period of time and then go back to eating and drinking by mouth. Others live with a gastrostomy tube for longer periods of time and, while they are rendered less mobile and more limited in their activities, they enjoy participating in conversations, reading, and other pastimes. IV lines have proven beneficial to many patients because they provide them with liquids at little pain or risk.

As effective as these forms of artificial nutrition and hydration often are, however, they can sometimes present distinctive burdens. Having a nasogastric tube inserted, for instance, can be uncomfortable. Once it is in place, if it moves and fluid enters the lungs, pneumonia can result. Infections, bleeding, and ulcers can also ensue from the use of these tubes over a long period of time. Because gastrostomy tubes must be inserted and removed surgically, they pose the additional risks that surgery presents. Socially, patients on feeding tubes tend to be more isolated from others, for they lose the sort of personal contact that comes with having people sit with them and feed them three times a day. This is a serious disadvantage of the use of such forms of artificial feeding.

IVs also can have certain drawbacks. Patients must have a needle stick, and this may have to be repeated periodically if the original site of the stick becomes inadequate. Conscious patients may be bothered by IVs and feeding tubes and may try to pull them out. If they attempt to do so, they may have to be restrained with bindings.

iii. Why has there been controversy about the use of artificial nutrition and hydration?

Different people view artificial nutrition and hydration in very different ways. Some see the provision of nutrition and hydration through tubes or IVs as a medical procedure in which manufactured chemicals that do not resemble food and water are inserted through an apparatus into the body. To them, this seems very different from feeding someone by hand with a spoon from a cup. They believe that using medical technology to provide food and fluids to those near the end of life, rather than allowing them to limit their food and fluid intake at their own pace, amounts to "force feeding." They also think that to decide against artificial feedings for those near death does not amount to starving them, for people ordinarily do not experience a terrible period of suffering when they stop eating near the end of life and die. Instead, they die a peaceful and comfortable death.

Yet others see the use of artificial nutrition and hydration in a very different way. They believe that using it to provide feeding supplements through tubes is similar to giving regular food by mouth. They believe that no matter what a person's condition, a feeding tube or IV should be used because it is contrary to Christian charity to deny food and water to any human being. They hold that not providing tube feedings amounts to starving people and fear that the person who dies from the lack of food and water in this way will suffer a miserable death.

Although both views can be found within the Christian community, the first appears to have gained greater acceptance than the second. The prevailing view seems to be that artificial nutrition and hydration are forms of medical treatment that patients or their surrogates can refuse.

iv. Is it painful to have artificial nutrition and hydration withdrawn near the end of life?

There is considerable testimony from doctors and nurses who work in hospice that those who do not receive technological feedings near the end of life die a comfortable death. It is not unusual for those who are near death to lose their normal appetite and to eat and drink less or not at all. Evidence suggests that this is not a painful occurrence and that it even contributes to the comfort of dying patients. Indeed, studies indicate that some near the end of life who accept artificial nutrition and hydration experience stomach discomfort and nausea. Studies also suggest that providing artificial nutrition and hydration to dying patients may be associated with medical complications.

v. If we decide not to use artificial feeding near the end of life, what sort of care is available for us?

When artificial nutrition and hydration are discontinued, this does not mean that all care for us must stop. This is the time to provide us with all available comfort measures. For instance, if we have a sense of dryness in our mouth because we cannot take liquids by mouth, this can be eased by giving us sips of water, ice chips, and mouth lubricants. We can also receive medication to relieve pain, shortness of breath, and nausea. Social support and spiritual counsel are especially important to us at this time. The goal now is that of hospice care—to keep our pain and suffering at a minimum and to allow us to have a good death.

vi. How can we decide whether to use artificial feeding when we are terminally ill or in the advanced stages of a disease?

The answer to this question depends on why a person can no longer take food and water by mouth. In some cases, patients have a temporary medical problem that can be overcome by the use of feeding tubes or IVs for a short time. Providing them with artificial nutrition and hydration can help to restore them to their previous condition. In situations of this sort, the benefits of using feeding tubes seem greater than their burdens, and it would be ethically sound to choose to have these tubes inserted.

However, sometimes patients can no longer take food and water by mouth because they are nearing death. When people enter the final stages of dying, they can have difficulty swallowing. This is considered by many practicing physicians to be a part of the process of dying and not a new medical problem. There is medical evidence that tube feeding at this time does not lengthen the lives of these patients but that it can add to their burdens. This is because hydration may create additional fluid in their throats and lungs and they may become more congested, swollen, and uncomfortable as a result. Some maintain that, in view of the burdens that can be created by providing artificial nutrition and hydration to those near death, it is ethically sound not to provide it.

Sometimes patients can no longer take food and water by mouth because they are in a confirmed irreversible coma or in a confirmed persistent vegetative state. (See Appendix A.) Medical science has no way of reversing these conditions or of bringing persons with them back to a point where they can relate to the community. So the question is whether to continue to use life-sustaining procedures to hold death at bay for them or to allow their condition to take its slow but inevitable course toward death. Answering this question is highly controversial.

Some hold that if a decision is made to stop the use of feeding tubes in patients in an irreversible coma or persistent vegetative state, this allows an already existing illness that cannot be reversed to take its natural course toward death. By withdrawing artificial feeding, the lives of those in these conditions, who have no hope whatsoever of ever recovering or of being able to relate to others, are allowed to come to an inevitable close. Thus, they believe that since these tubes will not reverse the underlying illness, it would be ethically permissible to decide not to continue their use for those in a confirmed irreversible coma or persistent vegetative state. This conclusion, they note, follows not only from the Christian view that we need not attempt to extend life as long as possible by medical means (see Section 4. b. above), but is also supported by the United States Supreme Court in the case of Nancy Cruzan, mentioned above (Section 3. c.). In that case, the court held that artificial nutrition and hydration may be withdrawn from a patient in a persistent vegetative state if the patient's previously expressed desire not to have life artificially prolonged meets a state standard of evidence.

Others, however, maintain that the condition of the person in a persistent vegetative state is not "terminal." This person could live for a long time in this condition. They are reluctant to decide against providing artificial feedings to him or her because that would allow death to come sooner. Indeed, some argue that what causes the patient's death is the withdrawal of artificial feedings, not the patient's underlying condition. This line of argument would seem to apply to the withdrawal of any life-sustaining treatment, such as respirators, resuscitation, and antibiotics, from patients who are not immediately dying. It takes a view that seems at variance with our ordinary view of what is means to cause death: that a person acts directly and intentionally to bring about death. (See Sections 5. e. and 7. b. below.)

Here is the story of how one person considered the pros and cons of using IV feedings and made a difficult decision about the use of a feeding tube for her mother.

Fran W. lived in a nursing home in a special unit for those with Alzheimer's disease. She could not move around much and needed assistance in going from her bed to a chair or to the bathroom. When her daughter, Susan, or a nurse's aide, tried to feed her with a fork or spoon, she would turn her head away. This alarmed the nursing home administrator and he asked Susan if they could start an IV line to provide Fran with concentrated nourishment. Susan consented.

When Susan returned after a work-connected trip two days later, Fran's arms were restrained with soft bindings and she wore a vest that, in effect, kept her tied in bed. Although her mother did not look as though she was in pain, Susan was dismayed, especially when Fran struggled to get out of the bindings that immobilized her. Susan protested to the nursing home administrator. He told her that her mother had tried to pull out the IV line several times since it had been inserted, and that they had put on the restraints to keep her from doing this.

Susan asked to have the restraints removed, and the administrator recommended that she speak with Fran's doctor. The doctor explained over the phone that the only way Fran could receive adequate nourishment was through an IV that was in place. Her arms had to be restrained so that she did not pull it out. Since the IV was not inserted permanently, Susan could have it removed if she wished. This would mean, however, that her mother would probably stop eating altogether and would die. Susan was terribly upset, for she did not want her mother to die, nor did she want to make a decision that she felt would contribute to her mother's death. She phoned the rector of her church, Bill C., who arranged to meet her at the nursing home the next day.

Bill said that he had seen other nursing home residents with Alzheimer's disease gradually stop eating and that it was always difficult to make decisions about whether to use feeding lines or tubes for them. Nourishment is not only necessary to remain alive, but it has great spiritual symbolism to Christians. Scripture offers accounts of divine feeding when God provides manna in the wilderness; Jesus multiplies fishes and loaves when there is not enough food for all to eat; and Jesus' disciples recognized his presence in the breaking of bread. Because we identify food with divine and human communion, we are reluctant to forgo it for those we love.

Yet Bill and Susan found significant differences between feeding someone through an IV line—the same sort of device by which medications and blood are provided—and feeding someone in person by hand. They examined several articles, written by hospice caregivers, that Bill brought along. These professionals observed that, in their experience, dehydration occurs naturally as we die. Those who are dying and refuse food and water do not suffer discomfort but have an easy and gentle death. One article noted that when elderly patients who are given artificial nutrition and hydration must be restrained so that they do not remove feeding tubes, their bindings could be a constant source of fear, discomfort, and struggle.

As they talked, Susan came to understand that Alzheimer's disease had put Fran on a downhill course toward death that could not be reversed. At this time, the disease had progressed to the point where her mother would soon die of it. Therefore, Susan faced the following choice: either to extend her mother's period of dying by artificial means, which would make Fran uncomfortable and unhappy, or to allow her mother to go in peace. If Susan stopped the IV line, she believed that she would not be the cause of her mother's death—Alzheimer's disease would be. Instead, she would be allowing her mother to go naturally in comfort.

After thinking it over for several days, Susan asked the nursing home administrator what could be done to make her mother comfortable if the IV were removed and Fran still did not eat or drink. The administrator said that they could provide Fran with sips of water and ice chips and would have staff attend to her so that she would not be alone when Susan was not there. Susan then called Bill to tell him that she was going to ask to have the IV removed. He offered to come over to the nursing home with her when this was done.

They met at Fran's bedside, and, after Bill and Susan offered a prayer for Fran, the IV line was removed. Fran continued to refuse food and water in the ensuing days and died peacefully a few weeks later.

Anonymous

This story reveals how difficult the decision to remove tube feedings can be. Because we associate food and water with necessary sustenance for us when we are well, it is hard to accept that a time can come when they can be more burdensome than beneficial. Susan gradually came to a decision that this time had come for her mother and she made the painful decision to stop artificial feedings.

Here is another story in which a decision about the use of artificial nutrition and hydration was even more difficult because of a difference of opinion between a family member and the nursing home administrator about what should be done.

> My mother, a sixty-seven-year-old widow, collapsed unexpectedly one day on our front lawn. Neighbors summoned an ambulance when she did not move or respond to them. They called me and I arrived at the hospital soon after she did. The emergency room physician told me she had suffered a stroke and that she was comatose. I was determined to do everything possible to help her to recover, so when she was discharged from the hospital after two weeks, I had her transferred to a nursing home that had an excellent reputation for its rehabilitative services.
>
> Mother improved. She returned to a semiconscious state and responded to stimuli a week after her admission. Three months later, however, she suffered another stroke and again became comatose. She remained in this condition for two years. During that time she received excellent nursing care and was nourished and medicated through a nasogastric tube. I visited her every day.
>
> After this two-year period, though, I began to reconsider my decision to provide every available medical measure for my mother. I thought that she would say she did not want to be maintained like this, if she could tell me her wishes. When I spoke to the nursing home administrator about removing the nasogastric tube, he adamantly refused. He said that no one in his nursing home would starve to death. My mother's physician said that she was in a persistent vegetative state with no hope of recovery. Using a tube for artificial nutrition and hydration seemed to him to amount to "extraordinary" treatment at this point. If the tube were to be removed, however, my mother would have to be transferred to another nursing home.

I called the rector of my church, who came to the nursing home to see Mother and me. She said that she, too, thought that it was right to remove the tube because Mother had no chance of recovery. Mother was beyond the point where humanly she could relate to God and others, and the rector believed that God was calling Mother home. She did not consider this "starvation," but the withdrawal of a medical treatment that could no longer accomplish its purpose—to restore Mother to conscious life.

A week later we transferred Mother to another nursing home. We had the nasogastric tube removed and had her provided with comfort care. She died two weeks later.

This was the most difficult decision that I have ever had to make. My mother and I had a very close relationship, and I desperately wanted her to return to consciousness. That was not part of God's plan, though. I know that she will tell me when I see her in heaven that I did what she would have wanted, could she have spoken for herself.

Jonathan Baxter

These stories illustrate how great the differences can be among people of good will about the use of artificial nutrition and hydration. That is why it is especially important for us to talk with our families, our priests, and our physicians before we make this choice. This can allow us to develop a sense of whether we want to use artificial feedings when we are near the end of life.

d. Accepting or refusing antibiotics

i. What are antibiotics?

Antibiotics are medications that either kill bacteria or stop them from growing. They are most commonly prescribed for bacterial infections, particularly those involving the lungs, throat, or middle ear. Different antibiotics may be used for different types of infections.

ii. What are some of the distinctive benefits and burdens of using antibiotics?

Antibiotics are often viewed as "wonder drugs" that can be administered simply and safely to overcome infections. Thus, we tend to assume that it is always beneficial to administer these drugs. For this reason, antibiotics are given routinely to nearly all patients with signs of infection. Yet the availability of a drug to treat infection does not resolve the question of whether we ought to use it to stop an infection. We must first consider whether administering such a drug can be disproportionately burdensome for some persons who are near the end of life. Let us explain how this can be.

Administering antibiotics is not always simple and without ill effects. It can be burdensome. Repeated injections and progressive loss of suitable injection sites can create pain and suffering in those who receive antibiotics for a considerable period of time. Furthermore, in some cases, it will not only be burdensome, but ultimately futile to use them to fight infection. For instance, some patients who experience a series of increasingly serious and painful reinfections undergo gradual and severe deterioration that ultimately leads to their death—despite the use of antibiotics. Thus, while administering antibiotics can provide a welcome and beneficial form of life-sustaining treatment for many patients, it can be a disproportionately burdensome act for others. These "wonder drugs," like other forms of life-sustaining treatment, can be withdrawn or not used when they would create great burdens for patients that are not outweighed by their benefits.

iii. How can we decide whether to use antibiotics when we are terminally ill or in the advanced stages of a disease?

We recall that we are not obliged as Christians always to sustain life by using every medical measure that is available. Therefore, we must consider whether the use of antibiotics would bring a balance of benefits to us in our particular circumstances or whether the use of this sort of drug would be disproportionately burdensome for us.

In many instances, antibiotics can overcome an infection and restore us to good condition. However, in others, their use may initiate what some call a "cascade" effect, in which one infection is overcome by antibiotics only to be succeeded by another infection and then still others. After each course of antibiotics for successive infections, the patient is left in worse condition and moves on a downhill course or on a "cascade" toward death. When this seems a strong possibility, we must ask whether we ought to allow the downhill cascade to start by providing antibiotics.

Some choose not to use these drugs in order to avoid the pain and suffering that successive infections can bring. They recall that in the days before antibiotics came into use, pneumonia used to be called "the old man's friend" because it allowed those who were frail and who could not survive much longer to die in peace and comfort. In some instances, when a person is near the end of life, a death from pneumonia or some other infection can be more comfortable than the death that would result from an underlying fatal disease, such as cancer. Yet there are cases in which treating an infection in those who are in poor condition and on a course that will lead to death would make them more comfortable in their remaining days. In those instances, it is appropriate to choose to use these drugs.

Here is a true story (in which the name of the patient has been changed) about how one relative decided whether or not antibiotics should be used:

> Carl Jurgen was an eighty-three-year-old retired gold merchant who was admitted to a nursing home due to declining mental abilities that prevented him from caring for himself. Although he could say a few words clearly, they had no meaning, and he was unable to relate to others. He sometimes interrupted the quiet of the nursing home with episodes of screaming for which no cause could be found. He was worked up for dementia, but no treatable condition could be found. The general picture of Mr. Jurgen at this time was of a frail, thin, severely demented man who took pureed food listlessly and slept much of the time.
>
> Carl had been a dashing figure throughout his life and had traveled widely across the world in the course of business. He had never married and had no children. His only living relative was a niece who lived nearby. She came by to visit him occasionally and was saddened by his situation.
>
> A month after his admission, Carl began to eat less and less solid food. Yet when his doctor examined him, he could find no new medical problem or abnormality. Laboratory tests showed that he had a marked anemia and his serum albumin was

reduced, indicating that his overall condition and nutrition were not up to par. Soon after, Carl developed a fever along with twitching of his limbs. He was sent to the hospital for treatment of these "seizures," and it was discovered that he had a bladder infection. This was treated with antibiotics and he was sent back to the nursing home. His niece and nurses at the nursing home found that his symptoms worsened after his return from the hospital and thought that going to the hospital had had a disruptive effect on him. Therefore, his niece requested that further hospitalization be avoided if possible and that he be kept comfortable.

Three weeks later, Carl would not eat at any mealtime and was very sleepy. He seemed to be in no distress. Tests ordered by his physician showed no abnormalities. His food intake remained poor for several days and he developed a fever. An X ray showed that he had a small area of pneumonia in his lungs.

Carl's niece spoke with his doctor about his long-term outlook. The doctor told her that antibiotics might be effective for this pneumonia but that there was a chance they might not. Moreover, his underlying condition could not be reversed. If this round of antibiotics did overcome this pneumonia, Mr. Jurgen would probably develop occasional pneumonias in the future and would live several more months, becoming increasingly weak until he died.

Carl's niece concluded that since her uncle was on a downhill course toward death, the most important consideration was how to allow him a peaceful death. She felt that having repeated infections would be extremely discomforting for him. Therefore, she decided not to have antibiotics used for his pneumonia and instead requested that he receive comfort care. This was done and Carl died a few days later. (Adapted from *Casebook on the Termination of Treatment and the Care of the Dying*, edited by Cynthia B. Cohen, Bloomington: Indiana University Press, 1988, pp. 70–75.)

e. If we decide to have life-sustaining treatment withdrawn from someone because it is useless or disproportionately burdensome, do we kill that person?

As we observed above, it is morally appropriate to withdraw or withhold treatment when (1) it does not provide a reasonable hope of success in sustaining life or restoring health or (2) it imposes a disproportionate burden on the patient. Thus, our intention in such circumstances is to remove a burdensome technology that holds little promise of meeting the patient's treatment goals. When we remove a life-sustaining treatment, we do not introduce a new and fatal illness but we allow an already existing condition to continue toward death. We do not kill, but we remove barriers to death that have proven useless or disproportionately burdensome to continue. Therefore, when doctors and patients agree to end treatment in such circumstances, they and we do not wrongfully cause death, but rightfully allow death to come.

f. If we decide to have life-sustaining treatment withdrawn, how can we cope with the personal impact this will have on us?

Once we decide to remove life-sustaining treatment, knowing that death is likely to follow, it can be very difficult to deal with the emotions that we and those we love experience. While we may feel relief that we will no longer have burdensome medical treatments, we and those we love will probably also experience anger, denial, and even guilt. Anger and denial may result from knowing that we will not have additional years in which to enjoy our families and our work. Guilt may surface because we might imagine that there must be something more that we can do or could have done to prolong life.

Our priests and other pastoral counselors can help us grapple with these concerns as we move toward death. They can help us express our feelings without judging us. We can ask them to assist us to plan our last days, deciding whom we want to be there, what in our lives needs forgiveness, what we fear most, and what we still need to do before we are ready to die. These religious counselors can provide the catalyst for our experience of peace, reconciliation, and hope at the end of life.

Here is another story that tells how one family that had approved a "Do Not Resuscitate" (DNR) order felt about their father's last days.

"Do not resuscitate!" Three simple words which, in the context of a human life that appears to be near the end, means "let this person die peacefully and comfortably."

A month before he died, my father, a past vestry member of an Episcopal parish, executed a "living will" and a durable power of attorney for health care. These two documents clearly expressed my father's wishes: the only healthcare treatment he was to receive when near death was medicine to alleviate pain; my mother was to make final healthcare decisions for him. I think the documents gave my father some comfort that his wishes would be honored, and they helped his family anticipate how some of the final decisions would be made. My father wanted to spend his last days on earth in the comfort of his home.

Notwithstanding these documents, the healthcare aides who assisted my father on a twenty-four-hour basis felt they would be obligated to call 911 if my father started to have extreme difficulty breathing or went into convulsions or some other form of extremis. If emergency personnel came to our house, they would likely perform traumatic and painful procedures on my father, and they would take him to a hospital for "extraordinary" treatment. These measures, we thought, would defeat the primary purposes of the two documents that my father had executed.

Therefore, I advised my mother, a lifelong Episcopalian, to have a physician sign a DNR order for my father. She did so, and I think we all felt that my father's wishes would be respected. I believe they were. Four days later my father died quietly at home in the presence of his wife and three children and in apparent comfort. May he rest in peace and may we all be able to die with such dignity.

Participating in the healthcare decisions for my father during his final days was for me, and for all the members of my family, a difficult, important, and solemn experience. It helped us to prepare for my father's death, to grieve, and to begin the healing process.

John S. Winder, Jr.

g. Discussion questions

1. Do you know someone who has decided not to have CPR and has asked to have a "Do Not Resuscitate" (DNR) order entered into his or her medical records? Why did he or she reach this

decision? How do you feel about it? What factors would be important to you if you had to decide whether or not to have CPR done?

2. Why might the question of whether to use artificial nutrition and hydration arise for someone who is near the end of life? Do you believe that the use of artificial feedings is always warranted? Or do you think there are times when it is morally appropriate not to use them? What reasons, feelings, and tenets of faith enter into your conclusion?

3. Have you ever heard the expression "Pneumonia is the old man's friend"? Why do you think people used to believe that? Do you think we should return to that view today and decide not to treat serious infections, such as pneumonia, in older persons near the end of life? Might this vary from person to person? Or would you hold that it is always morally necessary to treat such infections? Why?

4. In each of the stories presented above, the families found that the decision whether to use life-sustaining treatment could not be made quickly and easily. They needed time to accept that the person involved was near the end of life and could no longer benefit from treatment. Where did they find sources of help and strength as they made their careful decisions?

6

Caring for Those in Pain and Suffering

Although most of us need not feel substantial pain at the end of life, we are afraid that we will. Indeed, some fear this more than we fear death itself. It comes as a relief, therefore, to learn that health-care professionals today are reemphasizing the need to care for the physical, emotional, and spiritual discomfort we may experience in our last days. Doctors and nurses trained to use available pain-relieving measures skillfully can be called upon to diminish and alleviate our discomfort. Relieving pain does not necessarily alleviate suffering, though. To help us face the spiritual pain of suffering and assist us to reaffirm our relationship with God, ministers and pastoral counselors can offer us their support.

a. Does God send us pain and suffering as punishment for our sins?

When we experience pain and suffering during an illness, it is natural to ask, "Why?" "Is God punishing me?" "What have I done wrong?" We may have feelings of anger, abandonment, confusion, and guilt at these times. Yet we may also feel the tender, loving hand of God holding us close and recall that God does not willingly inflict pain on us. A prayer for those in trouble or bereavement in *The Book of Common Prayer* assures us of this. It reads: "O merciful Father, who has taught us in thy holy Word that thou dost not willingly afflict or grieve the children of men. . . ." (p. 831). We also recall the scriptural account of the man born blind, in which Jesus denied that individuals who are sick or disabled are being punished with illness for particular sinful acts of theirs or their parents (John 9:1–5).

One father expressed the following view about whether God punishes us by bringing us sickness and suffering near the end of life:

> I sat this summer beside my daughter's bed after she had had major spinal surgery. And I know with a deep certainty that illness cannot be the will of God. God does not punish our sins by giving us terminal disease as a sort of training tool. If we should not "do evil that good may come of it" then we can be quite certain that God does not do so. I do not know, I do not understand, why suffering exists in the world, but I am quite clear that it is not a bright idea, a nifty notion, on the part of God to make us shape up. . . . The gospel accounts of Jesus' ethics in relation to many forms of suffering are complex, but his response to illness is extremely straightforward: he heals . . . [and] he does so promptly and without question.
>
> God desires the wholeness and health of all the creation. That is God's purpose in creating it. That is God's purpose in redeeming it. (Sarah Maitland, "Is Health a Gospel Imperative?" in *Embracing the Chaos: Theological Responses to AIDS*, ed., James Woodward, London: SPCK, 1991, quoted in *Lent Day by Day*, 1998, St. Columba's Episcopal Church, Washington, D.C.)

Anglicans, however, do find a generic link between the misuse of human freedom and illness or misfortune. All creation fell; in Christ all creation is redeemed. Although it is not the primary will of God that any of us should suffer, we can view sickness and suffering as an opportunity to accept our participation in the human condition—both estranged from God and yet reconciled with God in Christ. Thus, the Anglican tradition teaches that we can regard sickness as an opportunity for the examination of conscience and a time to affirm our dependence on God. The letter of James (5:13–16) advises:

> Are any among you suffering? They should pray. Are any cheerful? They should sing songs of praise. Are any among you sick? They should call for the elders of the church and have them pray over them, anointing them with oil in the name of the Lord. The prayer of faith will save the sick, and the Lord will raise them up; and anyone who has committed sins will be forgiven. Therefore confess your sins to one another, and pray for one another, so that you may be healed. The prayer of the righteous is powerful and effective.

Anglicans, like all Christians, find in the life of Jesus—a life spent relieving pain and suffering in individuals—the revelation of a compassionate God. We know that God in Christ shares in our brokenness and pain as he embraces, consoles, and heals us when we suffer in ways beyond our expectations. We may come to accept suffering as a reminder of our solidarity with Christ and with other humans in their suffering, as well as of the unshakable assurance that we will not be abandoned by God.

b. Does the Christian faith require us to bear pain and suffering instead of alleviating it?

Suffering literally means to feel the press of something upon us, as when we suffer bad weather. Thus, in suffering, we experience external forces impinging upon us and come to recognize our limitations. We realize that we cannot on our own control our lives. Instead, we are God's. This is the truth that Job discovered when God appeared to him in the whirlwind (Job 38–42). It is the truth expressed by Jesus when he prays in the Lord's Prayer, "Your will be done" (Matthew 6:10). And it is the truth behind Jesus' prayer on the cross: "Father, into your hands I commend my spirit" (Luke 23:46). When we experience unavoidable suffering, as all in the human condition inevitably do, we can relate our suffering to that of Jesus and, through faith and prayer, see it transformed by God. Paul assures us that "the sufferings of this present time are not worth comparing with the glory about to be revealed to us" (Romans 8:18).

However, even though suffering may draw a person more deeply into relationship with God, God does not require us passively to bear all suffering that can be alleviated. Indeed, Christians are called to relieve suffering. God's mind about this is revealed in Scripture, where we find Jesus desirous of healing those suffering in pain or spiritual desolation. He heals those, like the hemorrhaging woman, who seek wholeness. He calls us to follow his compassionate way, alleviating pain and suffering—our own and that of others. Therefore, we are not required to bear pain and suffering when we can remedy it.

c. Should we remain silent about any pain and suffering we may have near the end of life?

Often we are hesitant to talk with our caregivers if we are in pain or if we are spiritually desolate near the end of life. We may feel that our pain and suffering are so private and so vividly present to us alone that we can't really describe them to others—so we keep silent. We are also reluctant to speak up because we don't want to seem like "complainers." As Christians, we may think that we should suffer in silence, offering our pain to God in prayer.

Yet doctors, nurses, and chaplains often say that our words and gestures give them important clues as to what sort of care would be most effective in easing any discomfort we may have. They observe that self-reporting by patients is central to the evaluation and treatment of pain and other discomfort. Further, they find that we vary a great deal as individuals in how we respond to pain and suffering and that care that is helpful to one person may not be appropriate for another. Caregivers need to know as much as possible about the pain and desolation that we may feel near the end of life so that they can develop an individualized palliative care plan with us to alleviate any distressing symptoms we may experience.

> Joe S. was reluctant to discuss his discomfort and isolation with his doctors and nurses. When he came down with pneumonia in the last stages of leukemia, he was sent to the intensive care unit of the hospital. Once there, he experienced pain, nausea, shortness of breath, and other distressing symptoms. Even worse, although he had often had a sense of the presence of God, he was having difficulty finding God in his current circumstances.
>
> When his doctors, nurses, and priest asked whether he was in pain or having any difficulties, however, he did not tell them about his pain and suffering. He had served in the Marines and felt that he would be a coward if he talked about his misery and discomfort to his doctor. Besides, he believed that Christ on the cross had set an example of bravery, and he was not going to succumb to weakness now. It wasn't until one of the resident doctors in the unit who had also been in the Marines, said, "You

must be feeling pretty bad," that Joe finally told him about how uncomfortable and anguished he was feeling.

The doctor recognized that Joe needed skilled care to relieve his pain, as well as sensitive spiritual counseling to address his sense of abandonment by God. He therefore called in the palliative care team of the hospital and the rector of Joe's church to work with Joe to ease his pain and suffering. The team provided Joe with morphine in doses that were sufficient to relieve his pain without rendering him unconscious. His rector, in praying Morning Prayer with him, read out loud Canticle 9, and Joe felt that God was speaking to him and his condition. Soon he was more comfortable and was transferred to a hospice unit for further palliative care.

Several weeks later, after saying his goodbyes to his family and friends and putting himself into the care of God, Joe died in peace. By breaking through his reluctance to be a "coward" and deciding to let his caregivers know how much he hurt and how abandoned he felt by God, Joe had a good Christian death.

Anonymous

d. What is palliative care and how does a palliative care team work?

Joe's doctor, in the story above, called in the palliative care team, along with Joe's priest, to help ease his discomfort and anguish. Palliative care is treatment that aims to relieve our pain and other distressing symptoms when we cannot be cured and to care for us so that our lives are as meaningful as possible. This form of care often includes personal support and counseling by a team of caregivers from various disciplines who have had special training in the evaluation and treatment of pain.

The team carries out a pain assessment with us. This includes asking us to describe our current pain, the way in which pain has affected our lives up to now, and what pain-relieving medications we have taken and with what results. The team may conduct a physical examination and do a general medical evaluation. Our emotional, social, economic, and spiritual concerns will also be considered by the palliative care team. Often the team works with a hospital chaplain or parish minister who has been on this path before with others and can help us step by step.

The palliative care team then develops a care plan with us on the basis of all of the information that we and those close to us have provided to them. This plan will often include the use of pain-relieving drugs for us. A plan for the use of morphine, for instance, would include instructions about how it will be administered to us, at what dosages, and on what schedule. Since it is easier to prevent pain than to bring it under control, the palliative care plan usually provides that analgesics, such as morphine, will be administered to us on a regular basis around the clock, rather than in response to our pain. The plan also provides treatment for bothersome symptoms we may have besides pain, such as fatigue, loss of appetite, nausea, constipation, inability to sleep, and depression. These may be responsive to treatment approaches that do not utilize drugs, such as massage, heating pads, ice applications, and relaxation techniques.

Moreover, a minister or pastoral counselor is often closely involved in the palliative care plan so that we can receive needed spiritual support and comfort during this time. Such spiritual care should be coordinated with our own minister. The palliative care plan is reassessed frequently with us by the palliative care team to ensure that we remain comfortable near the end of life. (See also Section 8. b. below on hospice care.)

i. What if we do not have access to a palliative care team?

If no palliative care team is immediately available, it is important for us to talk with our physician about what alternatives are available. Physicians are well aware that they receive more training in sustaining life than in treating pain. To remedy this, some have gained additional knowledge about pain relief and end-of-life care through refresher courses being offered to healthcare professionals around the country. Such caregivers can be of great help in treating pain we may have. Sometimes, however, we need even more specialized treatment from a medical consultant who specializes in pain relief. In that case, we should ask our physician to find one. Those who have no primary physician and need help in locating a pain specialist can get referrals from the American Cancer Society or the pain clinic in the anesthesiology department of the nearest major medical center.

ii. What help is there for us if our pain seems unrelievable?

A few of us may experience severe pain near death that cannot be alleviated by the use of pain-relieving drugs. In such rare cases, physicians can provide us with sedation so that we are not conscious of pain. Depending on our individual circumstances, responses, and wishes, we may choose to be sleepy for a few days, and then be more awake, continuing this cycle to the end. This sort of sedation is a last resort because it lessens the time of wakefulness that we have to spend with those dear to us before we die.

e. Why has there been concern recently about whether some near the end of life are receiving adequate treatment for pain?

Recent studies have revealed that those who are near death have not, in general, received adequate pain relief. There is growing recognition among healthcare professionals, patients, policy makers, and ethicists that the medical profession needs to do more to ensure that pain in terminally ill patients is not undertreated. To remedy this situation, we must understand why it has come about and what can be done to correct some of the mistaken beliefs underlying it. There is a host of reasons for the lack of adequate pain relief for dying patients.

For one, some doctors and families believe that dying patients will become addicted should they receive amounts of narcotics sufficient to relieve their pain. Therefore, they provide them with insufficient medication. A second reason is that some physicians fear that using pain-relieving drugs would depress their dying patients' breathing and hasten their deaths. They worry that this would be viewed as a form of killing or assisted suicide, practices that raise serious moral and legal problems. Third, many doctors and nurses recognize that they have not received training that equips them to assess and treat pain effectively.

Finally, economic and regulatory factors have led healthcare professionals to provide inadequate pain-relieving drugs to dying patients.

i. Will we become addicted if we are given large doses of narcotics near the end of life to relieve our pain?

The fear of addiction is a common one among family members with a critically ill patient in pain. For instance, Trish H. was seriously ill with ovarian cancer. When she entered the hospital, her doctor prescribed morphine on a regular basis to control the pain she had begun to have. Her husband, Sam, was concerned about the large dose of morphine she was receiving and worried that she would become addicted. Her parents, too, believed that Trish might become dependent on drugs, and they urged Sam to have their use stopped. Sam spoke to Trish's doctor about their concerns. She called them together and gave them the following information.

Drugs such as morphine and other narcotics are routinely prescribed for patients who are near death and in pain. It is rare for such patients to become addicted. They do not develop an intense craving for drugs and do not seek to find and use them in greater amounts than prescribed—typical responses of those who are addicted. According to some reports in medical journals, fewer than one percent of patients who receive narcotics for pain become addicted to them. Trish's doctor also pointed out that the concern about addiction was not a relevant consideration in Trish's case. She was near the end of her life and there was not sufficient time left to her in which to become dependent on drugs. The major concern at this point in her care was to relieve her pain and suffering by safe means. This is what they were doing when they provided her with morphine on a carefully measured regular basis.

ii. Is it wrong for physicians to provide us with pain-relieving drugs near the end of life if these might hasten our death?

The overwhelming majority of those who are near death and in pain can be made comfortable by the use of narcotics without dying sooner. A strange thing happens when we are given increased doses of narcotics that are carefully measured to control our level of pain—we build up a tolerance to these drugs. Although we may require larger doses of morphine to alleviate our pain as time goes on, the increased amount of the drug still has little effect on our breathing. This means that, contrary to what is commonly believed, the appropriate use of narcotics is not likely to depress our rate of breathing and bring about death sooner. Indeed, the use of pain-relieving drugs such as morphine can often extend, rather than shorten, our lives because they reduce our stress responses, help us feel less depressed, and make us more likely to accept food and fluids.

In some cases, however, an earlier death can result from the use of pain-relieving drugs. Moral theologians have concluded that giving such drugs for the purpose of easing pain, even when this accelerates the point of death, does not amount to killing. When drugs depress respiration in patients and thus lead to an earlier death, this is a side effect of using them, not the sole purpose of giving them. The beneficial effects of using such drugs— pain relief—exceed their negative consequence of shortening a life that will soon end. The General Convention of the Episcopal Church addressed this serious concern in a resolution adopted in 1994, in which it stated that

> Palliative treatment to relieve the pain of persons with progressive incurable illnesses, even if done with the knowledge that a hastened death may result, is consistent with theological tenets regarding the sanctity of life.

Christian ethicists see a distinct moral difference between giving adequate doses of drugs to patients to relieve their pain and giving overdoses of drugs to patients in order to end their lives. Giving adequate pain relief to the dying does not amount to a form of killing. A 1975 Anglican Working Group maintained, in *On Dying Well:* "There is a clear distinction to be drawn between rendering someone unconscious at the risk of killing him and killing him in order to render him unconscious." The Hastings Center, a well-regarded independent medical ethics research organization, stated in its *Guidelines on the Termination of Life-Sustaining Treatment and the Care of the Dying*, "Providing large quantities of narcotic analgesics does not constitute wrongful killing when the purpose is not to shorten the lives of the patients, but to alleviate their pain and suffering." Thus, if the use of narcotics to relieve pain and suffering should hasten death, this does not amount to intentional killing or to assisted suicide. Instead, it is an unavoidable and unintended side-effect of using these drugs.

Many doctors believe that they may open themselves to criminal charges if they provide large doses of narcotics to dying patients—even when these doses are clearly justified to relieve pain. Yet few physicians have encountered legal difficulties for giving proper doses of drugs to dying patients. Many of the states that ban assisted suicide are careful to exclude from the definition of assisted suicide the act of providing adequate pain relief to those who are dying. Moreover, as healthcare professionals become more knowledgeable about how to use pain-relieving drugs for those near death, they will establish a standard of practice that will protect them from legal charges of assisted suicide or intentional killing.

iii. What special efforts are being made today by doctors and nurses to treat our pain more effectively?

Doctors and nurses realize that by providing us with appropriate pain relief, they offer us a great gift—a slice of pain-free time in which we can put our personal affairs and our souls in order before we die. Recent reports of the undertreatment of pain and suffering among critically and terminally ill patients have spurred healthcare professionals to develop and increase programs of palliative care around this country. The American Medical Association has joined with a dozen other healthcare organizations to create a program for healthcare professionals that supports good palliative care for patients at the end of life. As part of this effort, a series of educational courses for physicians has been developed that is aimed at improving competence in comprehensive end-of-life care. These make appropriate treatment of pain in dying patients a high priority. Other professional medical groups, such as the American Pain Society and the American Society of Anesthesiologists, have developed practice guidelines for pain relief and palliative care. These tools encourage physicians to provide the amount of medication needed to counter patients' pain at the end of life.

iv. What economic and regulatory barriers are there to providing adequate palliative care to the dying?

Because palliative care is not always covered by healthcare insurance, we do not know to ask for it and institutions tend to overlook it. Some healthcare plans do not cover the cost of hospitalizing patients when they need this to control pain, nor do they cover home use of equipment such as infusion pumps that provide a steady stream of pain-relieving drugs. Thus, when we need specialized palliative treatment, we may find that it is not available to us unless we can afford to pay for it out of pocket. Or, we may find our health insurance does cover palliative care—but only if we are hospitalized. This was the case in the following story.

> Jan S. had breast cancer that could not be controlled and was hospitalized for pain. There she was given high doses of medicine intravenously to control her pain. Jan wanted to go home with a catheter inserted into her spine to dispense the pain-relieving medicine. This would have given her more time with her husband and children before she died. However, her insurance did not cover the cost of the catheter, so she had to remain in the hospital. Although it would have been less expensive to send Jan home, her insurance plan required someone as seriously ill as she was to be treated for pain in the hospital.
>
> Anonymous

A related problem is that state regulations that are designed to prevent the diversion of narcotics for purposes other than pain relief allow only limited amounts of prescription medications to be given to patients at a time. Some physicians are concerned that if they prescribe a higher dose of narcotics than some dying patients require, they will incur legal penalties or have criminal charges filed against them. As a result, they feel forced to provide lower doses of narcotics than they would otherwise want to give us, and we may experience pain that could have been relieved.

Efforts are being made to address these difficulties today. A report from the Institute of Medicine of the National Academy of Sciences urges that states and the Congress pass new laws to change current restrictions on the use of narcotics to relieve pain in dying patients. The recent decision to institute a new diagnosis code for palliative care by the Health Care Financing Administration opens the door to insurance coverage of end-of-life palliative care. Efforts are also being made in the legal and regulatory areas to make it clear that the standard of care for patients near death can include providing large doses of narcotics to alleviate pain and suffering. While it is important to stop diversion of controlled drugs for unauthorized uses, this should not interfere with doctors' prescriptions of narcotics for pain management in those who are dying. ■

f. Discussion questions

1. Sometimes we find it difficult to talk with others about our pain. Why are we reluctant to do so? What can we do to encourage people to share and describe their pain? How can we help them to address and ease that pain?

2. Have you or someone you know ever needed pain medication and not been able to get it? Or have you received it, but found that it was not very effective? How did you feel and what did you do? What does this section of the book suggest to you about what to do in the future should you encounter these difficulties near the end of life? What resources are available to those who are dying and who need relief from pain?

3. How can we help the person who says, "I am in such pain and it is not getting any better. It must be because my faith is not strong enough"?

4. Many Christian ethicists believe it is morally acceptable to give drugs to relieve pain, even if this hastens death. Do you think they are right? Why or why not? What scriptural passages or prayers can you think of that speak of God's desire to comfort and care for us when we are in pain and perhaps nearing death? Consider Psalm 23, Matthew 5:1–4, Matthew 11:28, Luke 4:18, Luke 10:29–37, Luke 16:19–30, John 3:16, and John 14:18. You may also want to read *The Book of Common Prayer*, pp. 453 and 462.

7

Bringing about Death:
Assisted Suicide and Euthanasia

A good death, we have observed, can be one in which a faithful Christian chooses to forgo life-sustaining treatment and to receive only comfort care. Some believe that if we are really to provide a good death for some patients, this is not enough. They maintain that the only way to assure some patients that they will have a death free from pain and suffering is to end their lives directly and intentionally. That is, they believe it is morally acceptable for individuals to choose assisted suicide and euthanasia. The traditional Christian view that these practices are wrong, they hold, needs to be changed.

Those who disagree with them acknowledge that human suffering at the end of life deserves a compassionate response. They maintain, however, that such a response should not involve assisted suicide and euthanasia. Instead, they believe that Christians are obliged to provide comfort care and pain relief to the dying, and that we are to keep them company as they enter "the valley of the shadow of death."

Just what are assisted suicide and euthanasia? Should we accept them as acts that are morally right for us to carry out for those near death? Do Scripture, the Christian tradition, and reason offer us a definitive position about the morality of these practices, or can Christians in good conscience reach different conclusions about this? Although we have always had the ability to commit suicide or request euthanasia in times of serious illness, as Christians, we have viewed these practices as wrong. Is there reason to change this position today? We explore these questions briefly here and recommend that those with a special interest in them read *Assisted Suicide and Euthanasia: Christian Moral Perspectives*, written by the Committee on Medical Ethics of the Episcopal Diocese of Washington and available from Morehouse Publishing at (800) 877-0012.

a. What do we mean by assisted suicide and euthanasia?

By *suicide*, we mean intentionally taking one's own life by one's own hand. In *assisted suicide* someone deliberately gives the person who plans to end his or her life the means with which to do this at the latter's request. For instance, if a son were to give his mother, who was in great pain from terminal cancer, a gun with which she proceeded to shoot herself, that would be an assisted suicide.

By *euthanasia*, we mean that one person causes the death of another who is terminally or seriously ill in order to end the latter's pain and suffering. Euthanasia requires the specific intention to end the other's life. Thus, were a husband intentionally to give his wife a lethal injection of a drug to end her suffering, he would be engaged in euthanasia.

b. Can we draw a moral distinction between assisted suicide/euthanasia and withdrawing life-sustaining treatment for those near death?

We sense almost intuitively that there is a moral difference between the practices of assisted suicide and euthanasia and the act of removing life-sustaining treatment that is not working to reverse our course toward death. As we noted above in Section 5, we accept it as moral to remove a life-sustaining treatment when it cannot achieve the goal for which it was begun—to reverse the patient's downhill course toward death—or because it is too burdensome. Thus, we found that it is morally acceptable to remove a respirator from a patient in the intensive care unit who is critically ill and in multiple organ failure when the respirator can no longer offer him the possibility of recovery. When doctors and patients agree to end treatment that is no longer effective or beneficial, they stop a medical battle they have come to realize cannot be won and allow death to come. They do not cause death in such circumstances. Instead they end treatments that are no longer effective, knowing that death most probably will follow.

In contrast, when assisted suicide or euthanasia is carried out, doctors, patients, or others intentionally perform an act, such as injecting a lethal dose of barbiturates, for the purpose of causing death. Those who act to provide assistance in suicide or to practice euthanasia do not end treatment, but directly end a life. The authors of *On Dying Well*, a 1975 report from the Church of England, observed the following:

> Euthanasia implies killing, and it is misleading to extend it to cover decisions not to preserve life by artificial means when it would be better for the patient to be allowed to die. Such decisions, coupled with a determination to give the patient as good a death as possible, may be quite legitimate.

Some argue that since the outcome can be the same in withdrawing treatment from a person who is near death and in assisted suicide/euthanasia—a person dies—there is no moral difference between them. They also claim that the intentions of those acting are the same: both intend to end the patient's life. Yet these acts are not necessarily the same. When physicians remove a respirator from a patient who is near the end of life, they do not cause death, but allow it to come. However, when a patient is given a lethal dose of a drug to swallow, death necessarily follows, usually quite soon. The connection between the second act and death is a cause-and-effect connection.

This alone does not fully distinguish between withdrawing treatment and assisted suicide/euthanasia. This is because the intentions of those performing these two different sorts of actions ordinarily are different. Those who remove a respirator from a person who is near death usually do not do so with the intention of bringing about the person's death. They do this with the intention of removing treatment that is useless, knowing that death probably will follow. Those who perform assisted suicide or euthanasia, in contrast, intend to cause death. They act in order to bring about death. The differences of causality and intention are significant moral differences that distinguish withdrawal of life-sustaining treatment from assisted suicide/euthanasia.

c. How have assisted suicide and euthanasia been viewed within the Christian tradition?

Christians today cannot avoid discussing the morality of assisted suicide and euthanasia. The issue has reached the United States Supreme Court and the practice of assisted suicide has been legalized in the state of Oregon. We look to the church, as the upholder of a moral tradition and provider of pastoral care, for guidance on this matter. This is appropriate, as the Christian tradition has addressed the question of assisted suicide and euthanasia across the centuries and has generally held that these practices are wrong.

i. What do the Scriptures say about the morality of assisted suicide and euthanasia?

Our lives are a gift from God that we hold in stewardship, we learn from Scripture. As the Apostle Paul asks, "Do you not know that . . . you are not your own? For you were bought with a price" (1 Corinthians 6:19–20). We therefore promise in baptism to follow Christ and obey God. The decision to end our life, whether by our own hand or another's, is not simply a matter of our own private choice. We turn to the Bible and the Christian tradition as guides to help us in following Christ and in making such choices.

Although the Bible does not specifically discuss suicide, it does express horror at the shedding of innocent blood. In Genesis, we find God holding Cain responsible for murdering Abel, and we read "You shall not kill (murder)" as the sixth of the Ten Commandments in Exodus. The Bible gives no indication that it is any more permissible to take our own lives than it is to take another's.

The Bible presents a few stories of suicides. For example, Saul, already wounded, killed himself so as not to fall prey to the Philistines (1 Samuel 31:1–6), and Judas hanged himself after betraying Christ (Matthew 27:5). In none of these stories does the Bible either condemn or condone suicide.

The Bible urges us to find hope and meaning in the midst of suffering and death. The Psalms again and again give voice to faith even in the valley of the shadow of death, and Paul assures us that "the sufferings of this present time are not worth comparing with the glory about to be revealed to us" (Romans 8:18). Indeed, Paul accepted his own suffering and death as a sharing in Christ's sufferings (Colossians 1:24; 2 Corinthians 1:5). His and other scriptural examples have led Christians to oppose suicide and euthanasia as practices that deny the redemptive power of God.

ii. What does the Christian tradition say about the morality of assisted suicide and euthanasia?

Christians have long taught that there are situations in which we should willingly give up our lives for others. Martyrs, following the Gospel of John, which says, "No one has greater love than this, to lay down one's life for one's friends" (15:13), have chosen to die rather than deny their faith in Christ. They have been venerated within the Christian tradition as powerful witnesses to the Christian hope for resurrection from the dead. Yet an important distinction was made in the early church between martyrdom and suicide. Martyrdom was approved because the end intended in the act was not the taking of life, but the honoring of something that was an important good, such as God or another person. Martyrdom was to be accepted but not sought, whereas suicide was consistently prohibited.

Thomas Aquinas expressed the classical position that suicide offends against nature because it contradicts our natural desire to preserve life. It also offends against the human community of which each of us is a part, and against God, who is the giver of life. This view became part of the mainstream of Christian thought. Indeed, opposition to suicide was so strong that for many centuries persons committing suicide could not receive Christian burial.

The Christian tradition has also rejected euthanasia out of respect for God's sovereignty as our creator and out of concern for the vulnerable, whose lives might be ended unjustifiably.

That tradition maintains that not even compassionate motives can justify taking one's own life or that of another. Christians have held that killing might be justified only in self-defense, in war against an unjust aggressor, and, for some, in capital punishment.

Yet there have been Christian dissenters from this tradition. In *Utopia*, Thomas More depicted an imaginary land where suicide and euthanasia were encouraged for those suffering from incurable illness and racked by unrelievable pain. Some argue, however, that the book is satirical and does not present a serious argument for such practices. The best-known Anglican to defend suicide is John Donne who, in *Biathanatos*, defined suicide so broadly that it included all cases of willing death, including Christ's. Thus, it is unclear whether Donne was an advocate of suicide as the term is commonly understood today.

iii. What does the Episcopal Church teach about the morality of assisted suicide and euthanasia?

The Episcopal Church adopted a resolution at its 1991 General Convention stating that euthanasia is wrong. That resolution suggests that assisted suicide would also be wrong. Resolutions adopted at the General Convention, unlike canons, are not binding. Rather, they provide one of several ways in which the Episcopal Church conveys moral teachings on a particular issue to help members form their consciences. The resolution reads:

> It is morally wrong and unacceptable to take a human life in order to relieve the suffering caused by incurable illness. This would include the intentional shortening of another person's life by the use of a lethal dose of medication or poison, the use of lethal weapons, homicidal acts, and other forms of active euthanasia. (See Appendix C. 2.)

The 1994 General Convention both reaffirmed and clarified this statement. Responding to the concern that the 1991 statement might not allow terminally ill patients to use pain-relieving medication that might hasten death, the 1994 General Convention added:

> Palliative treatment to relieve the pain of persons with progressive incurable illnesses, even if done with the knowledge that a

hastened death may result, is consistent with theological tenets regarding the sanctity of life. (See Appendix C. 2.)

This makes it plain that it is the intent to relieve pain that directs the moral act of giving drugs to those near death, and not the side effect of this act, hastening death.

d. What arguments do some Christians give for accepting assisted suicide and euthanasia as moral?

Modern medicine, with its new powers to maintain life, forces us to face circumstances that earlier generations rarely had to face. Some Christian theologians argue that medical technology has taken such great control of the process of dying that it is very difficult to die naturally. Therefore, they argue, if it is right, in some instances, to withdraw life-sustaining technology and let death occur to a person who is terminally ill it is also right to end the life of a person who is terminally ill but not on life-sustaining technology, directly. That is, in the latter case, they say that since there is no technology that can be taken away so that a person can die, we end that person's life directly. These thinkers can see no moral difference between withdrawing life-sustaining technology from a person near death and killing a person near death. If we allow one as moral, they say, we should allow the other. In their eyes, the morality of treatment withdrawal is no different from that of assisted suicide and euthanasia.

Those who favor assisted suicide and euthanasia further argue that God has given us the ability to make responsible moral decisions, and that such decisions include that of ending our lives when we are near death. Moreover, they would deny that the God who is revealed in the loving and compassionate person of Jesus wills us to endure the uncontrollable pain that can accompany dying. They point out that Scripture abounds with calls for mercy. Paul in 1 Corinthians 10:13 taught that God will not test us beyond our ability to bear but will provide a means of escape. They ask, could not death be understood as a means provided and allowed by God to escape from unbearable trial in some instances? It is thus faithful, as well as compassionate, they argue, to allow those suffering in these ways to exercise their autonomy and end their lives.

Proponents of assisted suicide and euthanasia also argue that Christian concern for the poor and vulnerable in society calls for the legalization of these practices. They point out that if assisted suicide and euthanasia were accepted by law, they could be available to all members of society, not just to those who have the resources and connections to circumvent customary practices. They maintain that open and strict regulation would protect the vulnerable from choosing assisted suicide or euthanasia because of outside pressures or mental illness.

e. What arguments do other Christians give for rejecting assisted suicide and euthanasia as wrong?

Those who reject assisted suicide and euthanasia believe that the powers of contemporary medicine do not create a situation so new that the traditional Christian position against assisted suicide and euthanasia must be changed. Those near death have always faced the possibility of a prolonged and painful dying and yet Christians have not resorted to ending their lives directly to avoid this. Our responsibility for making choices does not encompass a right to reject God's gift of life by intentionally taking our lives or those of others. These thinkers point out that we can refuse medical treatment that would prolong our dying and use methods of relieving pain and reducing the suffering sometimes associated with dying that earlier ages did not have. We are called by God to alleviate the pain that those who are near the end of life may experience, not to kill them, they argue.

Opponents of assisted suicide and euthanasia further maintain that there is a moral difference between stopping life-sustaining treatment for a person, knowing that death may come, and directly ending a person's life through assisted suicide or euthanasia. When we stop treatment that is no longer effective or beneficial for a person, we do not cause death, but step back and allow it to come. When we engage in assisted suicide or euthanasia, in contrast, we end a human life. When we kill a patient near death or assist that patient to kill himself or herself, that patient does not die from the underlying condition, but from the act that was undertaken specifically to end his or her life.

Moreover, opponents of assisted suicide and euthanasia maintain that these practices pose a great risk of harm to highly vulnerable members of our society—the dying. If assisted suicide or euthanasia were made legal and patients with serious illness could choose to kill themselves, strong pressure would be exerted on patients near death to kill themselves or have others do this for them. This is because, as efforts to contain the costs of medical treatment increase, efforts to lower the number of persons receiving medical care will also increase. Those near death will be urged to end their lives rather than continue to be a financial burden for their families and society. Eventually, they would find it difficult to answer the question, "Why aren't you dead yet?" No child of God should have to justify remaining alive.

f. Are there any exceptional instances in which some Christian thinkers who are against assisted suicide and euthanasia accept them as moral?

Some Christian theologians maintain that we should allow an exception to the prohibition against killing in certain rare, extreme circumstances. Such thinkers hold that in some situations our pain and suffering may become so intense that it would be morally acceptable for others to kill us or assist us in suicide. The example often given is of a truck driver who is trapped in a fiery wreck with no way to escape. Rather than allow this person to suffer a terrible death, it would be morally admissible for a passerby to kill him or to assist him to commit suicide, they believe. A loving, compassionate God does not will such an excruciatingly painful death, they hold. Similarly, God does not will us to have a period of dying that is characterized by unrelievable and intense pain and suffering. Thus, they maintain, we are morally warranted in providing assisted suicide or euthanasia in such circumstances—but only as a last resort.

Most instances of terminal illness, however, are not similar to the unusual case of burning to death. They differ in the degree of pain and suffering involved or the nearness of death for the person. Therefore, these thinkers do not believe it generally would be morally acceptable to commit suicide or ask another to kill us when we experience pain and suffering as part of the normal course of dying. Instead, they would call for better use of the means available for taking care of such pain and suffering.

g. How can we resolve our differences as Christians about the morality of assisted suicide and euthanasia?

All sides of the Christian debate about the morality of assisted suicide and euthanasia share certain values: the duty to relieve human suffering, the obligation to respect individual autonomy and the ethic of the Christian community, and the need to respond to the call of Christ to protect the vulnerable. There is common ground among us. Acknowledging this can help us to move on, in a spirit of community and trust, to discuss those areas that we view in differing lights. We can gain a better understanding of why those who differ from us believe what they do and where we may share additional common ground. Moreover, those who take different positions on the issue of the morality of assisted suicide and euthanasia can join together to promote a clearer understanding within our society that caring for the dying must encompass a greater effort to end pain and suffering of God's creatures near the end of life. ■

h. Discussion questions

1. In your view, are there conditions or circumstances that would justify the use of either assisted suicide or euthanasia? Are there any circumstances in which you might consider one of these practices? What role would your faith play in making such a decision?

2. How would you respond to a friend or family member who was sick and asked you for help in ending his or her life? Why? Do you think that providing adequate pain relief and good palliative care to that person would lead him or her to a change of mind? What do you think should be done if a person's pain seems unrelievable?

3. Paul accepted his own suffering and death as a way of sharing in Christ's suffering (2 Corinthians 1:3–7 and Colossians 1:24). Because of this, the Christian church has believed that he provides a model for those who are opposed to assisted suicide and euthanasia. Do you think he provides such a model? What similarities and differences are there between Paul's suffering and his choices and those of a patient with terminal cancer or in the last stages of Alzheimer's disease? How do you believe God is present to these patients? What comfort, strength, and hope does that give you?

8

When Death Finally Approaches

When we make the difficult choice not to use or continue life-sustaining treatment, this usually opens the door to the appearance of death. At this time, we want to consider how we can care for those we love who are dying and also how we wish to be treated as we near the end of our lives. Therefore, we discuss here not only ways of providing comfort care but ways of coping with the difficult emotional and spiritual issues that may arise when we are dying. Our hope is that this will assist us each to realize our vision of what it is to die a good Christian death.

a. What questions should we (or our family and friends) ask caregivers about our care near the end of life?

Most of us spend our last days in a hospital or nursing home. There are certain questions we or our families and friends can ask of those taking care of us in these institutions so that we can understand and participate in our care. Just by asking some of these questions we can spur caregivers to consider whether they are providing appropriate treatment and whether they can improve our care. Moreover, the answers we receive will help us to plan our care and to decide whether to remain within the institution or to transfer to another facility or to home care.

- Who will be responsible for my care? At this institution, is there a specific staff person assigned to each patient to whom that patient can turn to for information and help?

- Has the staff been specifically trained to care for dying patients? Is there a palliative care team that will help with symptom prevention and the alleviation of pain?

- What sort of treatment plan will be established for me? Will I be involved in developing it? Will it take into account the preferences that I have expressed in person and in my advance directives?

- If I do not have advance directives, will the institution help me to find a way to develop them?

- Does the institution have an active ethics committee that provides ethics education for personnel and is available to patients and families making difficult decisions?

- What are the institution's policies about the removal of life-supporting technologies such as respirators? artificial nutrition and hydration? Do these policies take into account the need to reduce grief for all involved when life-supporting technologies are removed?

- Does the institution provide basic supportive care, such as appropriate nutrition and hydration, skin and mouth care, treatment for shortness of breath, and care for anxiety and other symptoms?

- If I come from another culture and English is not my primary language, what provisions are there to allow me to make my needs and wishes clear to English-speaking persons?

- Is social, emotional, and pastoral counseling available for me and my family?

- Does the institution have arrangements with home care agencies, hospices, nursing homes, and other organizations that assist dying patients so that I can be transferred to one if necessary?

- Is there a staff person who can locate bereavement support groups and other resources for my family when I am gone?

b. What is hospice care and how can it assist those who are nearing death?

Hospice care is care designed to help those whose condition does not respond to treatment and who are near death, as well as those who have decided not to seek further treatment for an advanced condition. Its goal is to provide those near the end of life with physical, emotional, and spiritual support and assistance so that they can live fully and comfortably while controlling pain and other discomforting symptoms. Hospice also offers social and spiritual support to patients, their families, and their friends during the period of dying and the process of grieving that follows.

To be admitted to hospice care, we must be *terminally ill.* When an illness is clearly in its final stages and there is no way to reverse it, a person is said to be terminally ill. However, there is no agreed-upon period of remaining life for the person to be considered terminally ill. Medicare regulations, for instance, put the length of time at six months or less. Other groups set it at a year. It can be difficult to declare that a person is close to death because of the great uncertainty that often surrounds this. In some instances, we don't know that a person is near death until he or she takes his or her last breath—and then it is too late to provide comfort care. Physicians, therefore, must use their experience and their best judgment when they project that a person is terminally ill.

Many of us, however, will not die of a disease that has a clear end point. Instead, we may die of a slow-moving chronic condition that has no predictable point at which death will occur. Thus, we do not fall into the category of terminally ill. When this is the case, we should ask our caregivers to provide us with the aspects of hospice care that are relevant to our situation, even though we are not considered terminally ill.

People tend to wait too long to enter hospice programs because they don't want to accept that they are dying. Moreover, some physicians are not aware of the existence of hospice programs or of their benefits and are therefore reluctant to discuss them with patients near death. Many patients, families, and doctors don't want to admit that the patients are dying until they are very close to death. Thus, the average time spent in hospice care is only about two weeks. That is a very short period of time, especially when we realize that an earlier admission to hospice would have provided comfort care sooner. The Christian call to recognize when it is our "time to die" means that we must face the fact that we are dying and take steps to move toward death in peace and comfort. Consequently, we should ask our physician about hospice, rather than just wait until he or she mentions it, so that we can receive this important form of care near the end of life in good time.

i. How does hospice work?

Hospice care is generally offered at home, but it is also provided in nursing homes, hospitals, and in-patient hospice units. When we receive hospice at home, care, consultation, and support are available to us twenty-four hours a day, seven days a week. Most home hospices stress the need for a relative or friend who can serve as a primary caregiver for us. In nursing home hospices, hospice caregivers assist the staff, observing and supporting us and our family and providing any extra assistance needed. When hospice care is given to us in a free-standing facility, specially trained staff carry out the hospice approach.

At the core of hospice care is an interdisciplinary team that provides comprehensive and continuous care. This team usually includes our personal physician or another physician, registered nurse, social worker, counselor, dietitian, and volunteers. Our parish minister or other religious advisor is often among this group. The team varies, however, depending on our needs.

Hospice care has several components that include:

- a consultation service by physicians and nurses with special training in pain control and supportive care
- therapies designed for control of our symptoms
- consideration of the needs of families, encouraging visits and ensuring privacy
- attention to our spiritual concerns, which may include reconciliation with self, family members, and friends

In a hospice setting, we participate in those activities we choose to enjoy. These may include having visits from close relatives and friends, finishing up "old business," and writing or revising a will. Preparation for death means, in part, "closing the loop" on matters large and small that we have always intended to take care of but somehow never gotten around to doing. Hospice provides the time and the support to allow us to do this. (See also above, Section 6. d. on palliative care.)

ii. When is it time to look into hospice care?

It can be difficult for us and for our families to accept that the time has come to inquire about hospice care. Here is how one family that included a member who was professionally affiliated with a hospice foundation decided that the time had arrived.

My father was diagnosed with lung cancer at a very young sixty-five years of age. He had no symptoms at all until severe pain in his hip led him to seek medical help. He was diagnosed with an advanced case of lung cancer that had already metastasized to his bones. Recovery was not expected.

Dad's treatment started with radiation therapy, which began to take its toll on him. Recently, our family had cared for an uncle who had died from lung cancer, and the effects of rigorous cancer treatments were clearly emblazoned on our minds. Images of Uncle Bob haunted us as we thought about ways to help my father with his struggle.

After radiation treatments, Dad decided against chemotherapy. Later, however, he chose it in search of a little more time. He hoped to see his son and daughter-in-law give birth to his first grandchild, an event a few months away. During this period of treatment, his hipbone shattered and he was in a life-threatening condition. Fortunately, and we thank God for this blessing, he survived hip replacement surgery. Of course, the cancer continued to spread and it was clear that his time on earth was limited. His doctors suggested additional chemotherapy. His earlier chemo treatments, however, had taken a terrible toll on him, and so he chose against this final round. At this point, we decided to bring hospice care into our home. It was important to all of us that he remain at home and that he be comfortable and free from pain in his remaining days. We wanted a good level of pain relief and physical comfort, yet we wanted him free from drug addiction.

Hospice was the answer to our prayers. What's so important about the hospice concept of care is that they look at the entire family and care-giving network, not only the "patient." They help you deal with the medical situation, as well as everyone's spiritual and emotional needs. We had access to professional nurses, social workers, health aides, clergy persons, and other support people.

As a family, we had time to spend with Dad while he could still communicate with us. He wasn't hooked up to machines in some far-away place. Hospice brought so much life to the days that remained. Those quality days, free from extreme pain and discomfort, were a blessing from God. The death of someone you love is always a tragedy, but hospice put us in a place where we knew we could survive it. Hospice even followed up and stayed in touch with us through that first difficult year after Dad's death. There is no question in my mind that God was taking care of all of us through the resources that hospice care gave to my entire family.

Jon Radulovic

iii. What sorts of questions should we ask about a specific hospice program before we decide to enter it?

You will probably want to learn whether the hospice program you are considering will meet your needs. You can ask some of the following questions of its administrator:

- What are the criteria for admission?

- Who will be responsible for my care? Will I be informed about this?

- How will my preferences be accommodated? Will a record be kept of them?

- What role do families play in patient care at this hospice?

- What internal and external resources are available to provide twenty-four-hour physical and emotional care, spiritual support and counseling, and practical care for me and my family?

- What education has the staff had related to end-of-life care? Has the staff received training in palliative care and symptom relief?

- How is physician support for patient care organized? Can my personal physician continue to treat me after I enroll in this hospice?

- If home hospice care proves insufficient for me, what arrangements can be made for hospital or nursing home care?

For further information about hospice care, you can contact The National Hospice Organization, 1901 N. Moore Street, Suite 901, Arlington, Virginia 22209. Phone: (800) 658-8898 or call HospiceLink at (800) 331-1620.

c. How can we prepare for death?

It is our hope that we will not die unexpectedly or unprepared. Yet sudden death is not an uncommon event. Jeremy Taylor, the seventeenth-century Anglican moralist mentioned earlier, asked in *Holy Dying*, "And how, if you were to die yourself? You know you must. Only be ready for it by the preparation of a good life, and then it is the greatest good that ever happened to thee." Even when we are in good health, we can take steps to prepare for our own deaths. Although it may seem difficult to address questions concerning our own death, it is a gift to our loved ones for us to do so.

Those of us who know that we will die soon have sufficient reason to prepare for death. We can begin by asking our priest, religious advisor, family member, or friend to talk and pray with us about the end of life in this world and the life to come. Helpful and comforting services can be found in *The Book of Common Prayer.* These include the "Ministration to the Sick" (p. 453), "Ministration at the Time of Death" (p. 462), and "Reconciliation of a Penitent" (p. 447). In these services, we will find prayers for comfort, forgiveness, healing, grace, and strength. Some of the biblical passages listed in them can also be of immense help. An especially meaningful passage is from the Gospel of John, 11:25–26, where Jesus says: "I am the resurrection and the life. Those who believe in me, even though they die, will live, and everyone who lives and believes in me will never die."

This is also a time when we can reminisce and share memories with those close to us, going over highlights of our lives together. Many people find that they want to resolve differences with those whom they may have hurt or who have hurt them when they near the end of their life. We can also take this opportunity to disclose practical information to our family and friends about day-to-day things that they will need to know when we are no longer with them.

We may decide to draw up a "living will" or durable power of attorney for health care, if we have not already done so, to make sure that our family and friends understand whether we want life-sustaining treatment or special forms of care. Many will find the book *Before You Need Them: Advance Directives for Health Care, Living Wills and Durable Powers of Attorney* of assistance at this time. It was developed by the Committee on Medical Ethics of the Episcopal Diocese of Washington and is published at a modest cost by Forward Movement Publications, 412 Sycamore Street, Cincinnati, Ohio 45202. Phone: (800) 543-1813. When life-sustaining treatment is to be removed, many people have found helpful an Episcopal service, "A Form of Prayer at a Time When Life-Sustaining Treatment is Withdrawn," that can be found in the second part of *Before You Need Them*. This is the time to plan for the funeral service, if we have not done so already, choosing our favorite biblical passages and hymns. This sort of planning can be our final gift to our family and friends.

The widow of an Episcopal priest tells this moving story of a good Christian death:

> "I anoint you with this oil in the name of Our Lord and Savior, Jesus Christ, beseeching Him to fill you with His grace that you may know the healing power of His love."
>
> These words, spoken by my husband, Paul, as he anointed all those who came to God's altar seeking healing of mind, body, or soul in their lives, were spoken in faith. Paul believed in God's grace and in God's healing power—Paul believed in miracles.
>
> Thus, when Paul was diagnosed with a malignant brain tumor, it was in faith that he and his family and friends prayed for a miracle, a miracle that Paul would be restored to that wonderfully vibrant and joyful man that we loved so dearly. Paul loved life and he sought God's presence in all that surrounded him. A humble man, he found fulfillment in serving God in the priesthood and in the love of his family.

It was impossible to conceive of life without each other. The next two weeks were spent in shock and disbelief. The days were filled with brain biopsies. When the first was inconclusive, we held onto hope that perhaps the tumor was benign. But the second biopsy showed the tumor was definitely malignant and not in the hoped-for early stage, but advanced.

Paul accepted the diagnosis with strength and grace, allowing himself to be open to every possible medical means for treating the tumor. Visits and consultations with some of the most prominent physicians in the field ensued. *No*, the tumor could not be treated with a Gamma Knife, as it was too large. *No*, the tumor was not operable, as it was in an area of the brain that was too vascular and that controlled vital functions. *No*, there was no clinical trial or protocol available. We could see in the eyes and hear in the voices of the physicians the gravity of the situation. All agreed that standard radiation therapy was the only course available that might arrest or shrink the tumor and "buy some time."

Radiation therapy was begun three weeks after Paul's diagnosis. During this period, he lost his ability to walk or even turn on his own. We continued to pray and were lifted up in prayer by hundreds of friends. All of those who prayed were channels of God's love, uplifting and engulfing Paul and filling him with a strength of spirit that was a wonderful witness to all. We celebrated Thanksgiving with our family and continued therapy. Paul continued to decline and was now confined to a hospital bed in our family room. As we entered Advent, he wanted to begin to prepare the house for Christmas and delighted in visits from his children, godchildren, and friends.

On December 8, Paul underwent his final radiation treatment. It was evident that Paul's condition was deteriorating. A follow-up CT scan revealed that the tumor continued to grow. On that day, Paul made the difficult decision to stop treatment and to live his death as guided by the Spirit. He asked my help in doing this, as "one final gift of love." He hoped to create a space where he could return to the God whom he so loved in sure hope and faith that we share in the resurrection of our Lord and are indeed heirs of that everlasting kingdom. He wanted only palliative medical care, no resuscitation, no life support; he wanted us to be present with him and comfort him.

It was a difficult gift to give, one that could not be given alone. I was encouraged by the help of a hospice team, our children, our godchildren, and our friends. Paul assured all of us that God was very present to him, and for all of those who gathered around his bed day and night for the next four days that presence was tangible in each other. As we ministered to Paul's physical needs and comfort, we prayed and read the psalms.

Paul died on December 12, surrounded by that perfect love that casts out all fear. Our home was filled with music and children, and next to Paul's bed the Christmas tree was bright with light. Never before have I had such an awareness of the communion of saints. It was Advent, a time of hope and waiting, a time of preparation. Paul's waiting was over and his life transformed. His request for "one final gift of love" was returned to us in full measure by his powerful witness of faith. He will truly live on in the hearts and minds of all who loved him.

Judy Singer

d. Should we consider donating organs to someone in need when we are near death?

Donating organs or tissues to others can save their lives. Some people believe that donating these parts of themselves to those who can use them after they are gone gives their death special meaning. They see it as an act of Christian charity to offer what has been called "the gift of life" to others who are in need. That is why we and our families should consider the possibility of giving some of our organs and tissues to others after we have died.

Organs and tissues are not taken from patients until after it has been confirmed by physicians that they have died. Not everyone can donate organs and tissue to others, for these body parts can deteriorate while we are still alive or even after death and become unsuitable for use by others. Therefore, if we would like to contribute them, it is wise to give consent while we are still alive and to leave it to medical professionals to assess whether our organs and tissue are usable by others after we have died.

Some may be concerned that efforts to save our lives will weaken if the staff knows that we are willing to donate our organs and tissues to others. Usually, however, a transplant team becomes involved with us only after other physicians who have been caring for us determine that we have died. The separation of those who give us care while we are living and those who remove our organs after death is intended to protect us from a hastened death for the purpose of organ donation.

If we serve as organ or tissue donors, information about us is kept confidential; it is not revealed to those who receive our organs or tissues unless we have indicated that we want them to have this information. There is no financial cost to us or to our families for this sort of donation. Further, no one is paid for our organs or tissues, because a federal law prohibits their sale.

We can indicate that we are willing to become organ and tissue donors by filling out a donor card and keeping it in a safe place, perhaps attached to our advance directives. Most states allow us to note that we are organ donors on our driver's licenses. We should then let our families know that we have taken this important step. This is especially important for organ and tissue donation, as the permission of the family is usually sought before these body parts are donated after our death. It is also a good idea to tell our primary care physicians and our priests about our decisions to donate this "gift of life." If, for any reason, we change our mind about this sort of donation, we can destroy our donor cards or notify the state licensing bureau that we wish to change the statement about donation that is on our driver's licenses.

For more information about organ donation, contact the United Network for Organ Sharing at 1100 Boulders Parkway, Suite 500, Richmond, Virginia 23225-8770. Phone: (888) 894-6361 or (804) 330-8500. Website: http://www.unos.org.

e. How might we feel and respond as someone we love faces death?

It is emotionally wrenching for those who will survive to let go, even though we know that the one about whom we care deeply has no reasonable hope of recovery. It is not unusual for us to feel conflicting emotions at such times: we may want the person we love to live, but at the same time may hope that he or she will die so that the suffering will end. We may find it difficult to speak of these emotions and to share them with those dear to us. Doing so, we may fear, will make us appear callous or selfish, uncaring or inhuman. It is important to realize that it is not wrong to feel anger, guilt, and resentment about the fact that one whom we love is dying. We all have such emotions; none of us is unique in this respect. Fortunately, we can express our anger and work through it so that we can continue to care for the person we love. No one can pretend that coping with anger is easy. We need to explore the reasons for it, express it, and leave it behind, for continuing to nurse anger can be destructive and divisive, and of little help to anyone.

Here are the reflections of a respected rector of an Episcopal church in Washington, D.C., about feeling angry with God about tragic events in our lives.

> There are a lot of things in this life to be angry with God about. Birth does not always work out. Death is needlessly painful. We do the right things for the right reasons and end up in a big mess. There are lots of things in life for which we might be angry with God, that will leave us upset and frustrated with God. How many people do you know whose relationship with God, the church, and worship came to an abrupt halt after a death, tragedy, or some kind of suffering? They could not put the burden of their anger down. They could not set aside the barrier that their bitterness had put up. They could not forgive God for what they experienced and for how they feel about it. It is important to be able to forgive God, to set our anger aside, to lower the barrier our frustration creates. If we cannot forgive God then we must remain cut off from God. That is how important it is.
>
> Forgiveness is not just about right and wrong. God may well be right. . . . No doubt there is some great plan that I have not been privy to that would make sense of much that I experience as senseless. That does not matter. When something makes me angry, I am the one with the anger. I am the one who must let go of it. If God's action or Jesus' word leaves me with a bitter taste, then I have to wash it out. If my feelings constitute a barrier between me and my Lord, or me and you, then I am the one who must keep it open. That is what forgiveness is. . . . I thank God for a relationship deep enough for forgiveness to be necessary and strong enough for it to be possible. Amen. (Francis H. Wade, "Forgiving God," in *Companions Along the Way* [Chevy Chase, MD: Posterity Press, 1996], pp. 19–20.)

Some of us may feel guilty at this time because we imagine that there must be something more that we can do or could have done for the person dear to us who will soon die. It is not unusual to feel frightened, helpless, and worried about how to care for him or her. We may also be concerned that we will feel lonely and have nothing to live for once our loved one leaves us. Moreover, financial worries may press on us. All of these are natural concerns and emotions that, as human beings, we must go through. We should not put on a brave face and smother these feelings. Instead, we should talk them over with someone we trust, a good friend, clergy person, or healthcare professional.

i. Is it wrong for us to desire death for someone who is near the end of life?

It can be difficult to sort out our desires and intentions from the complex and often conflicting feelings we may have when we, or those we love, are near death. Yet it is important personally and pastorally to realize that it is not necessarily wrong for us to desire a quick death for someone dear to us who is dying. We may desire death for a person we love because it involves an end to his or her pain and suffering or because it is an entry into eternal life. Such a desire is a compassionate and loving one.

Having such a desire does not mean that we would bring about the death of one dear to us. We are not the helpless victims of our desires and can decide against acting on them when this would be wrong. Our intentions can control our actions in circumstances when they conflict with our desires. Thus, when we give narcotics to someone who is dying, we may intend to relieve his or her pain, not to bring about death—even though we may desire that the person die. We may pray for death for the person and yet not act with the intention of killing him or her.

ii. In what ways can we care for someone who is dying?

The best care we can provide for those who are dying is to be present with them. We can stay in place with them and God, who never leaves us alone in our helplessness. Those near death have a great need for intimacy and contact with people who love them. They need to be heard and touched and to feel that we sympathize with them. We should assume that they can hear everything that we say, even though they may seem unconscious. We can ask those who are clearly conscious, "How can I help you?" "What's this like for you?" "What worries you now?" "Is there anyone you'd especially like to see?" "Is there any unfinished business you want to take care of?" And we can even say, "I don't know what to say except that I love you." Sitting together, holding hands, hugging, crying, laughing, praying, talking, and listening are all gifts of presence we can give. These actions have a healing power that transcends the body. They are ways in which we can be God's hands and heart.

This is a time when our relationship with the dying person can become richer and our love even deeper. Differences can be resolved, old feuds set aside, and new meanings found for our lives together. Perhaps we will see love in a new light and realize how petty most of life's squabbles are. Perhaps we will learn about understanding and reconciliation, sacrificial caring and the immense strength we have within us. In years to come, we may well look back on these last conversations with gladness about what we were able to do and wonder at what we learned about ourselves and the one we love who has died.

When we accept the challenge of caring for someone who is dying, we are not merely doing our Christian duty. Indeed, we are doing more than committing ourselves to easing pain and suffering, more than sitting sadly by the bedside. We are dedicating ourselves anew to the God of love, who is ready to guide and strengthen us as we care for the one we love until he or she is finally enfolded within God's arms.

iii. Should we talk about death to one dear to us who is dying?

If we try to protect the one we love from the reality that he or she will die, we may miss meaningful conversations that can make this time so precious. It can be important to talk about death with someone who is dying; however, it is not always easy to do. Paul Tournier, a physician, observes in *A Listening Ear* that "people are well aware that they are going to die, that they must die, and yet we are afraid of talking about it to the dying person. We think we are sparing the person's feelings, but it is our own feelings we are afraid of." Talking about a person's impending death can free that person to discuss his or her concerns and hopes. It can open the door for us and those dear to us to an even closer and more meaningful relationship.

Yet such talk should not be forced on those who do not want to enter into conversations about their impending death. One person who read an earlier draft of this book made the following comments:

> This is a very complex subject. What about people who can't deal with the fact that they are dying? What about those who refuse to give up hope? My father and I spoke extensively about financial affairs and other practical matters, but he never spoke about dying per se. His physician asked him to sign a "Do Not Resuscitate" order but never discussed dying at that time! Some people simply recognize that they are dying but do not discuss it.

Each of us has to gain a sense of whether the person dear to us wants to talk about dying or simply wants us to be there to keep him or her company. We should try to open the door to such conversations so that the person we care for realizes that we are willing to do this and has the opportunity to gain a sense of peace and completion at the end of life.

iv. What should I do if the person who is dying asks me a tough question like "Why me?" or "Why is God doing this to me?"

As we face death, we are confronted with our vulnerability, our finitude, and our utter inability to change our situation. We may have the helpless feeling of being forsaken by God. Some may feel that their situations are parallel to that of Christ, who spoke of being forsaken on the cross. As humans, we are aware that we are not granted immunity from untimely, random, and undeserved death. Some respond to this "crisis of finitude" by turning away in bitterness and despair, not only from God but also from friends and family. Some may lose hope of any meaning and joy in their life and death. Others open themselves to the future, trusting in God's grace and love to carry them through death into eternal life.

We can suffer great spiritual pain if we have mistaken beliefs about how God works in the world. Many of us have a shadowy concept of God and are unsure of how God views us and relates to us. Some believe that they have become ill because God is punishing them for something they have done or have not done. Others believe that God has abandoned them. Even those who have a deep faith in a loving, compassionate God may feel that God seems further and further away as they are dying.

As we begin to pray about, think through, and live with our situation, we recall that God does not deliberately impose illness, pain, and suffering on us as a punishment. Indeed, the Bible witnesses to a God who "does not willingly afflict or grieve anyone" (Lamentations 3:33). We look to a God of love, exemplified in Jesus Christ, and in him we see God reconciling and restoring the sick and the troubled—not capriciously wreaking vengeance on them. When we face the anguish of knowing we will die or the tragedy of losing someone we love, God suffers with us. There is a grace in this suffering that passes all understanding that we may come to know more fully as we come to rest in God. (See Section 6. a. and b. above for further discussion of whether God punishes us by sending us sickness.)

When some of us who are dying ask, "Why me?" we may simply be expressing our grief and anger, rather than seeking an explanation. Any answer, no matter how theologically sophisticated, may be perceived as an unwillingness to face the depth of our pain and an attempt to shove it away with a pat response. In such situations, others do not need to have an answer for us. Instead, they need to be there and to tell us that they understand our pain and anguish. In this way, they can express God's love and compassion for us.

f. How can clergy and other advisors help us during this time?

When serious illness invades our lives, it is time to put aside our pride in being self-reliant and allow others to help. Religious advisors can assist us as we move toward death. They can accompany us as we plan our last days, as we decide with whom we want to share these days, what in our life needs forgiveness, what we are most afraid of, and what we still need to do before we are ready to die. Members of the clergy and other pastoral counselors can provide us with the catalyst for an experience of peace, reconciliation, and hope at the end of life.

g. What sort of care would be helpful to receive after someone we love has died?

After religious services, which have heralded the passage of the one we love into new life, we may experience a letdown and feel bereft. Some who are bereaved say that they have a sense of emptiness and feel as though there is a "hole" inside them. Such grief is not a sign that we lack faith. *The Book of Common Prayer* observes, "Jesus himself wept at the grave of his friend. So, while we rejoice that the one we love has entered into the nearer presence of our Lord, we sorrow in sympathy with those who mourn" (p. 507).

Friends, family, and clergy can allow us to "tell our story" and be heard at this time. They can listen to us and hear our pain with no other agenda than to walk with us through it, accepting without judgment where we are in our grief. Others can help us by just being present with us, accepting us, and empathizing with us. Grief counselors say that before we are healed, we may have to grieve many times. They tell us that grief may return just when we think we have gotten through it. Some of the books listed in the bibliography at the end of this book may be helpful in the process of grieving.

We may also find that a support group at church or in our community that is focused on people who are grieving can be especially meaningful after someone we love has died. Such groups can recognize that not all people experience death and grief in the same manner. They can encourage us to share our grief and accept the reality of our loss at a pace that is right for us. They can help us to bridge the gap between life before and after the death of our loved one, helping us to look forward to new life and hope in the future.

Professional caregivers also need aftercare. They, too, are touched by the death of a patient and need support. Words of thanks, cards, and notes can be of great comfort to these professionals, who are committed to exhibiting hope and compassion to dying patients and their families on a daily basis. ■

h. Discussion questions

1. If you were told that you were terminally ill, to whom would you want to talk about this? What would you want to say? What would you want to do? How would your faith inform your response?

2. Dying today may seem far removed from dying in biblical times because we have access to so many medical advances. Yet human responses to the approach of death are timeless. You may want to read some of the following biblical accounts and discuss the similarities and differences in dying then and now:

> Genesis 48:1–2, 8–11, 15; Genesis 49:1, 28–33; 1 Kings 2:1–10; Matthew 27:46; Luke 9:44–45; Luke 22:39–46; Luke 23:39–46; John 17:13–26; John 18:4–11; John 19:25–27

What was the response of these biblical figures to their impending deaths? of those close to them? What was important for them to take care of or resolve before they died? What guidance do you find in these accounts for dying in the contemporary context? What comfort?

3. Do you know someone who received hospice care? What sort of treatment and visits did he or she receive? Did hospice help this person to achieve reconciliation and a peaceful death? Would you recommend it to a friend?

4. "I don't know what to say" is the lament we sometimes express about spending time with those close to death. It can seem a frightening task for which we lack the skills. What can we say to those who are near the end of life that will bring them comfort? Need we say anything at all? What have you found helpful at such times?

5. We often feel that we need to keep a stiff upper lip when someone close to us dies and not allow our tears and sorrow to show. After all, we may reason, the person dear to us is out of pain and at peace, and so we should be glad. But death is still painful to us, even when we anticipate it and accept it. Read p. 507 of the Order for Burial in *The Book of Common Prayer* and then turn to John 11:32–36, where Jesus responds to the death of his friend Lazarus. How do these passages speak to you? to others who grieve?

9

How Our Healthcare System Affects Those Near the End of Life: Justice and the Christian Community

Our healthcare system is changing rapidly today. We have begun to realize that we do not have the resources to do all that it is possible for medicine to do and at the same time carry out other activities that are important to our society, such as providing education and safety. Consequently, we must make tough choices about what sorts of health care to provide to those who are ill. This new approach is leaving many of us bewildered about what kind of care and services we can expect when we are near the end of life. (See Appendix B.) In this section, we briefly consider how pressures to contain costs are affecting care for those near the end of life. We go on to offer positive steps that those nearing death can take to improve their care in the face of our current healthcare system. Finally, we address certain related questions of justice that are important to the Christian community.

a. What sort of care is available for those sixty-five or older who are near the end of life?

Medicare, the publicly funded healthcare program that covers those who are sixty-five and older, provides hospice benefits for those who are near the end of life. These include nursing care, home health aides, physician supervision, prescription drugs, light housekeeping assistance at home, and respite care for family members. To qualify as terminally ill and receive these benefits, patients must have a prognosis of six months or less to live, as determined by a doctor. This can be helpful to those with a specific known terminal condition, such as cancer, who can be given a fairly reliable prognosis in terms of months. However, this requirement does not always allow Medicare patients with other serious chronic illnesses, such as congestive heart failure or chronic obstructive lung disease, to receive hospice-type care. This is because it is more difficult to give a specific prognosis of length of remaining life for such conditions and to know when patients have six months or less to live. A new MediCaring demonstration project of Medicare makes hospice care available to those with chronic conditions from which they will ultimately die who will live longer than six months. If the project shows that this way of caring for such patients is an improvement over current ways of doing so, it will be adopted by Medicare.

Currently, those on Medicare who do not have a prognosis of six months or less must rely on regular Medicare benefits. These pay for nursing home care for short convalescent periods (approximately twenty days) after hospitalization but do not cover long-term care. They also provide limited coverage of outpatient medications and supportive services. Many who are sixty-five or older who are not designated as terminally ill, therefore, must cover such services and medication out of their own pockets or receive help from family members. The use of home care and home health agencies for Medicare beneficiaries has been growing rapidly in recent years, and this may reduce distress and dysfunction for many whose time of death is difficult to predict.

b. What sort of care is available for those under sixty-five who are near the end of life?

Those under sixty-five who are near the end of life must rely on health insurance plans or, if they are uninsured, see if Medicaid is available for them. Many health insurance plans, however, do not cover nursing home or hospice care for those under sixty-five who are dying. Further, the responsibility of employer-sponsored plans that do provide for such care may end when employees exceed the maximum coverage allowed or must resign their jobs because of their illness.

This leaves many below sixty-five who are near death with few options for care outside the home unless we have sufficient funds of our own to pay for it privately. We may therefore elect to receive care at home, since managed care plans (see Appendix B) will often provide home treatment. This means that a family member must be at home to care for us and to admit the home-care worker for visits. Relatives who have jobs, however, may not be able to afford to stay home for more than a few weeks to care for someone who is dying.

Some under sixty-five who are near the end of life may qualify for Medicaid benefits for hospice care. Medicaid is a program funded by the federal government and administered through the states for persons of limited income who need medical care.

c. What sort of care is available for those near the end of life who have no healthcare insurance?

Some of us do not have any sort of healthcare insurance because we are retired, homeless, or unemployed. Others may be without such insurance because they cannot afford the premiums, are not offered insurance by an employer, or are employed in a contract or part-time position that does not provide health benefits. Most in these straits cannot afford to purchase health insurance privately.

Some of us in this position may qualify for Medicaid. If we are not eligible for Medicaid and have no healthcare insurance, we may be able to receive medical care through neighborhood clinics set up by charitable organizations or through the emergency room of the nearest hospital. Charitable clinics are few and far between. Emergency departments are required by law to stabilize us when we enter in a critically ill state. If we are expected to remain seriously ill after we have been stabilized, the institution may make efforts to qualify us for public insurance or to arrange a transfer for us to a public facility. However, we may find that we are discharged from an emergency department while we are still sick—even if we are terminally ill, but will not die imminently—and have nowhere to go for treatment.

The social work department of a healthcare institution may be able to find out whether what are known as "Hill Burton" funds are available to assist us. Many institutions that were built or renovated in the early 1950s obtained government loans under the Hill Burton Act. In return, these facilities promised to provide free medical care for those with limited means. Their obligation may have transferred to new owners if the facility continues in use. Therefore, it is possible that care at such an institution may be available. Again, this is not a common situation; such funds may not be available to us even when we are near the end of life.

The public health nurse from the County Health Department or the Visiting Nurse Association can assist us in seeking affordable or free health services. Local or state chapters of disease associations may be of assistance to those without insurance who need health care at home. The American Cancer Society, for instance, may provide limited funds for medications, dressings, equipment, and other care supplies. Other associations may loan us large equipment, such as hospital beds, bedside commodes, and walkers.

For many without healthcare insurance who are near the end of life, however, the hope of receiving adequate care is dim.

d. What financial concerns does end-of-life care raise for those who manage our healthcare system?

We spend an increasing amount of money on care at the end of life in the United States. This is because our population is growing and aging and, consequently, there is an increasing number of people who are at the end of life. Moreover, the general costs of medical care have increased and end-of-life expenses have increased along with them. The price of care at the end of life has attracted special attention among government policy makers because much of it is publicly financed through government programs such as Medicare and Medicaid. Private insurers are also concerned about these costs because they provide many of the "Medigap" policies purchased by older people. Because of this, efforts are under way to decrease the cost of end-of-life care and to do so, hopefully, without diminishing its quality. (See Appendix B.)

e. Will efforts to curb costs lead to limits on end-of-life care?

Some are concerned that the physical, emotional, and financial burdens of curbing the costs of health care fall especially heavily on those who are dying. They fear that current cost-containment policies may discourage providing appropriate palliative care for those near death who are in pain and suffering. They also believe that these policies may lead to discharging patients from healthcare institutions "quicker and sicker," thereby allowing death to come too soon. Although many welcome the chance to go home when they are near death, others who are discharged early may not have sufficient time to organize home palliative care and other forms of care. Further, some may need certain kinds of pain relief that can be provided only in a hospital; they will not receive such care if they must leave the hospital early. Current financing arrangements, therefore, may have a negative impact on those who are near death.

Medicare administrators and other insurers are becoming concerned about this problem and have been reviewing and revising current policies in order to ensure care of good quality to those near the end of life. They are giving somewhat greater attention to pain relief and to improved terminal care. Along these lines, a Committee on Care at the End of Life of the Institute of Medicine recommended in 1997 that healthcare organizations should do the following:

- Make palliative care available wherever dying patients are cared for—in hospitals, nursing homes, patients' homes, etc.

- Promote more timely referrals to hospice care for patients who can benefit from it.

- Encourage patients' personal physicians to continue to be involved in their care after they enter hospice.

- Provide more complete discussion between caregivers and patients about patients' diagnoses, prognoses, and care objectives so that they can plan ahead and prepare for dying.

f. What do we owe to those near the end of life who have been made vulnerable by poverty, disease, disability, or age?

A Christian ethic calls us to take special care of the sick, the poor, the oppressed, and the underprivileged. God's concern for those in such plight is a recurring theme in Scripture. In Deuteronomy, we read: "Since there will never cease to be some in need on the earth, I therefore command you, 'Open your hand to the poor and needy neighbor in your land'" (15:11). Eight centuries before Christ, the prophet Amos railed against a society in which people who got into debt might be sold into slavery for no more than the cost of a pair of shoes (Amos 8:6). Jeremiah said of Josiah: "He judged the cause of the poor and needy; then it was well. Is not this to know me? says the Lord" (Jeremiah 22:16). In the Old Testament, to "judge" the oppressed means to deliver them.

Jesus' concern for the poor and outcast shines throughout the Gospels. It is shown by his acceptance of lepers; his table fellowship with tax collectors, prostitutes, and other assorted sinners; and in several of his parables. Those who assist the hungry, thirsty, naked, sick, and imprisoned, Jesus assures us, enter eternal life, for in helping these persons, they help Christ (Matthew 25:45–46). The early Christians took Jesus' example to heart. Acts 2:44–45 records that "all who believed . . . had all things in common: they would sell their possessions and goods and distribute the proceeds to all, as any had need." Indeed, "there was not a needy person" among them (Acts 4:34).

Caring for the vulnerable and dying is one of the significant ways in which we can respond to the call to emulate Christ. The community has a responsibility to assist those who cannot take care of their own health because of poverty, age, or disability. We are not isolated individuals who must always stand alone on our own two feet, regardless of circumstances. Instead, we are dependent on one another and bound out of the love of Christ to help one another meet our basic needs. Christians have sought over the centuries to make real the words of Paul in 1 Corinthians 12:7 that "to each is given the manifestation of the Spirit for the common good." The early Christian example makes it clear to us today that we owe those who are near death decent medical and nursing care, along with companionship, as their lives in this world draw to a close.

g. How does Christianity call us to distribute health care in a just way?

The Christian injunction to imitate Christ means that we should base the distribution of basic health care on the need of each person, not on the ability to pay. Thus, the Christian view is that when disease or disability impairs our basic well-being and capacities for normal functioning, the community has a responsibility to intervene, making a decent minimum of health care available not only to those who can afford it but also to those who cannot. Thus, the General Convention of the Episcopal Church has asserted the right of all persons to medically necessary health care. (See Appendix C. 3. See, in particular, Resolution A057 passed by the 1994 General Convention.) To fail to provide a decent basic level of care so that we can effect cost savings contradicts a Christian ethic of health care.

Yet our current system of health care is based on our ability to pay. It presumes that health care is a commodity that is no more significant than any other product on the market. As Christians, we should be wary of this approach because it ignores the special moral significance of basic health care. Bouma and his fellow writers declare:

> It is appropriate to distribute many things, including items from cookies to cars, according to the ability to pay. Distribution according to . . . [ability to pay] frequently creates an incentive for productivity and creativity which can ultimately advance the interests of everyone in society. But even the most ardent capitalist acknowledges the injustice of distributing some things according to this standard. Nearly everyone agrees, for example, that to provide police protection only to those who could pay for it would be unjust, and that to provide basic education only to those who could purchase it would be unfair. It is our judgment that the provision of at least a basic

level of medical care is more like providing police protection and education than like providing Oreos and Oldsmobiles. (Hessel Bouma, Douglas Diekema, Edward Langerak, Theodore Rottman, and Allen Verhey, *Christian Faith, Health, and Medical Practice*, William B. Eerdmans Publishing, Grand Rapids, MI, 1989, p. 162.)

Basic health care is a social good of moral importance. A Christian understanding of justice bases the distribution of that good on our need. Justice, however, does not demand that each of us have access to every single medical treatment and technology that is available. Society cannot afford to provide everyone with every treatment that they want in every circumstance. However, justice requires that each of us receive at least a decent basic level of health care. What constitutes a decent basic level of care is often disputed, but we believe it includes at least adequate care at the end of life.

Moreover, according to a Christian ethic, those who can pay for health care have a responsibility to contribute to the care of those who cannot. The parable of the Good Samaritan calls us to help our neighbor in need of medical and other assistance. Although we have undoubtedly worked hard to earn money to pay for our own care, we have not achieved financial security wholly on our own. We are indebted to the community, which has offered us such supportive structures as education, representative governance, and protection against violence, as we have pursued our goals. And we are indebted to God, who has given us such gifts as life and love. We can repay some of the debts we owe the community and God by contributing to the common good in proportion to the wealth we have received. We have a responsibility to ensure those who are sick a decent level of care and relief from pain and suffering. This is essential to what it means to be a Christian and a member of the human community.

Thus, those with financial means have a responsibility to support a healthcare system that provides treatment and services for those who have been made vulnerable to ill health by poverty, disease, disability, or age. Those who are better off, however, should not simply take over responsibility for the health care of those who are sick and poor. They also have an obligation to minimize the conditions that lead to ill health, so that individuals will be better equipped to take responsibility for their own care. At the very least, the provision of basic health care should be a priority of society for those who are at any age or stage of life.

It is a well-known fact that our current healthcare system does not provide a decent minimum of health care for all who need it, particularly those who are near the end of life. Moreover, it has few standards—and no national standards at all—for measuring the quality of care. A major overhaul of this system is needed in order to be consistent with a Christian approach to caring for the sick. Christians can begin that process in the following ways:

- by seeking the establishment of panels in HMOs with patient representatives that review disputed cases

- by urging that a commission of health caregivers and patients be established to work toward developing national standards for measuring the quality of health care, especially at the end of life

- by urging sanctions against health caregivers who fall short of the standards established by that commission

- by insisting on a funding stream to cover the care of the 30 million uninsured people in our country

Such measures would at least provide a start toward a healthcare system that is just and compassionate.

h. How can the Christian community become more active in ministering to those who are near the end of life?

There are many resources in our communities that could be made more available to those who are approaching death. Church groups might develop a list of resources that are available to dying patients in the local community, not only from healthcare institutions but also from churches, other charitable organizations, support groups, and agencies serving special populations, such as older individuals or people with disabilities. To get an idea of what sorts of resources could be included in such a list, see Appendix D, "Resources for Those Near the End of Life and Those Close to Them."

Christian groups and individuals could also start or join groups that provide nonmedical supportive services to those who are ill. Some programs that are funded by federal, state, local, or private sources deliver meals, provide transportation, and offer "respite" care for family members to assist in the care of older people and those with disabilities. ■

i. Discussion questions

1. Can our current healthcare system be modified to meet the needs of those near death who are vulnerable to neglect? How would you change it so that the poor and vulnerable receive responsive care? If you believe our current system is too broken to be fixed, with what sort of system would you replace it?

2. What do you think is a decent basic level of health care that should be provided to all, whether or not they can pay for it? Would it include eye care, dentistry, cosmetic surgery, organ transplants, palliative care, trauma care?

3. What might be done so that those who are terminally ill don't feel they have a "duty" to die to relieve financial pressure for their families?

4. If you were asked to contribute to a Healthcare Bill of Rights for the Terminally Ill, what would you recommend that it include? Why?

5. What steps can you take in your own family and your own community to reach out to those nearing death?

10

Final Reflections

As we plan to make our picture of a good Christian death become a reality, we envision certain things that we wish it to include. We see it as a period when our treatment choices, as children of God granted freedom and responsibility, are honored. We picture our process of dying as a time when we respect the value of the life God has given us, even as we accept that our time to die has come. For some of us, that means that we see our lives beneficially prolonged by medical powers for a while. For others in different conditions and circumstances, it signifies that our lives are not gravely burdened by continued treatment. Our picture of our dying is one in which we are as free from pain and suffering as our situation will allow. Those who are close to us are present, for a good Christian death, as a good Christian life, is one that we experience in the company of others. To be with loving people who are willing to listen to and respect our hopes, our fears, and our wishes, and whose presence brings us comfort, is the true mark of such a death.

Finally, this picture of a good Christian death is one in which we commend ourselves to God and offer a prayer of thanksgiving for our lives. It is a picture in which God does not allow sickness and death to have the last word. In it, death is conquered by Christ, who swallows it up in victory (1 Corinthians 15:54). Thus, even as we die, we affirm that:

> As for me, I know that my Redeemer lives
> and that at the last he will stand upon the earth.
> After my awakening, he will raise me up;
> and in my body I shall see God.

I myself shall see, and my eyes behold him
who is my friend and not a stranger.

For none of us has life in himself,
and none becomes his own master when he dies.
For if we have life, we are alive in the Lord,
and if we die, we die in the Lord.
So, then, whether we live or die,
we are the Lord's possession.

(Book of Common Prayer, p. 491) ■

Appendixes

Appendix A. Distinguishing Several Sorts of Prolonged Unconsciousness from Brain Death

Advances in medicine now allow us to sustain many physiological functions for years in persons who are permanently unconscious. Deciding whether to remove life-sustaining treatment from these persons has been fraught with difficulty. At times, it has been so hard to reach a consensus about what to do for these unresponsive patients that families or institutional administrators have gone to court. These difficulties have arisen, in part, because there has been confusion about what permanent unconsciousness is, how it differs from being dead, and whether those in this state should be treated. Therefore, we present the following discussion of "prolonged coma," "persistent vegetative state" and "brain death" to assist those of us who must make decisions about the use of life-sustaining treatment for persons dear to us who have been unconscious for a prolonged period of time.

1. "Prolonged coma" and how it differs from a "persistent vegetative state"

Some persons are in a prolonged coma, while others are in what has come to be known as a "persistent vegetative state" (PVS). Persons in either of these states still have some brain function and therefore do not meet the criteria for "brain death," but they have severe brain damage that renders them unconscious and unable to function in many ways.

Both prolonged coma and PVS are caused by brain damage, but they differ in certain respects. Persons in a coma seem asleep and utterly unaware of the world around them. Their eyes are constantly closed, and they do not show a sleep-wake cycle. In

115

contrast, those who are in PVS appear to be awake, and they have a sleep-wake cycle; however, they give no meaningful responses to their surroundings. Their eyes open periodically and they occasionally "make faces," shed tears, or even laugh. These are reflex actions, however, rather than knowing responses to the world around them. Both of these conditions can result from such causes as traffic accidents, falls, gunshots, cardiac arrests, drug overdoses, and brain disease. Which state a person falls into depends on how severely his or her brain has been injured and which part of the brain has been harmed.

The lower part of the brain, the brain stem, leads to the spinal cord and controls certain basic bodily functions, such as breathing, heartbeat, and reflexes. The upper part of the brain, the cerebral cortex, controls thinking, perception, awareness, and emotions. Persons in a coma have severe damage to both the upper cortex of the brain and the brain stem. Yet they may respond to treatment and recover consciousness. In general, comatose persons who survive begin to awaken and recover gradually within two to four weeks. Those who do not recover enter PVS.

Persons in PVS have lost the higher cerebral powers of the brain, but their brain stem remains intact, preserving their breathing and reflexes. They can remain in this state indefinitely. Whether they recover any of the functions they have lost depends on the cause of their condition, how long it has lasted, and their age. Recent studies have shown, for instance, that no patient diagnosed with PVS at one month following a heart attack has recovered lost functions; however, it may take up to six months of observation before PVS can be considered irreversible in a person who has suffered a head injury. The American Neurological Association Committee on Ethical Affairs maintains that PVS can be diagnosed in patients with "a high degree of certainty by well-defined criteria." Once PVS has been diagnosed firmly, recovery is rare. The American Neurological Association Committee states:

> While there have been occasional reports of recovery concerning persons who spent many months or years in a PVS, such data are fragmentary, the number of such well-documented

cases is very small, and the outcome has usually been one of persistent severe disability.

Thus, those in this condition have little chance of recovery, and if they emerge from it they do not regain their normal functions. The most common cause of death for those in PVS is an infection, such as pneumonia.

2. The meaning of "brain death"

"Brain death" differs from prolonged coma and from PVS. What is it and why have we needed to develop a special way of diagnosing when a person is dead in some situations? Our new technological powers give us greater control than ever before over the time when we die. Indeed, we can use these powers to extend life for such long periods that at times we have difficulty in determining just when a person is dead! Doctors used to declare a person dead when he or she stopped breathing and had no heartbeat. Today, however, they can use medical technology to keep breathing and heartbeat going, even though a person has no remaining brain function at all. Such a person is said to be "brain dead." A person in this state breathes and has a beating heart only because machines are performing these functions. Sadly, this individual will never again perform these functions on his or her own because the brain is totally destroyed. "Brain death" is permanent. There is no possibility that a person in this condition will return to life. His or her brain will never function again.

The person who is "brain dead" is considered legally dead according to the laws of all states in the United States. These laws usually follow a model statute that standardizes the point at which a person is declared dead. The model law was developed by the National Conference of Commissioners on Uniform State Laws, the American Bar Association, the American Medical Association, and the President's Commission for the Study of Ethical Problems in Medicine. Entitled the "Uniform Determination of Death Act," it reads, in part, as follows:

> An individual who has sustained either (1) irreversible cessation of circulation and respiratory functions or (2) irreversible cessation of all functions of the entire brain, including the brainstem,

is dead. A determination of death must be made in accordance with acceptable medical standards.

The central considerations in determining "brain death" are that the person (1) is unreceptive and unresponsive to others, (2) cannot breathe spontaneously, and (3) is in an irreversible condition. To these criteria, physicians usually add that there must be evidence of overwhelming brain damage or of disease that affects the brain, such as trauma, cardiac arrest, or stroke. Before the criteria for brain death are applied, doctors must use appropriate therapeutic measures to try to correct the patient's underlying illness. No drugs that depress the central nervous system should be present in the patient's system for thirty-six hours before death is declared. Further, two physicians must agree on the diagnosis of "brain death." The experienced clinician today can diagnose brain death with an extremely high degree of certainty by looking at the electroencephalogram reading and such signs as whether the pupils of the eyes are responding.

It is important to recognize when a person is "brain dead" for several reasons. First, we need to have an accepted point in time when a person's life is said to be ended so that we no longer use medical procedures on his or her body in futile attempts to bring the person back to life. Families need to know when a beloved relative is dead so that they can grieve for a time and then move forward with their lives. Second, many legal issues, especially those that have to do with a person's estate, depend on having a specific time at which a person is declared dead. Third, a person may have wished to donate his or her organs to others in need, and this cannot be done until the individual is clearly declared dead.

Appendix B. The Changing Healthcare System and Managed Care

Our healthcare system is undergoing a vast transformation. The costs of health care have increased steeply in the last twenty-five years and this, in turn, has increased the share of our national resources devoted to it. Consequently, expenditures on health care threaten to divert resources from other areas of our life as a society that are also important. In response, government and healthcare insurers are introducing new ways of controlling and reducing healthcare costs. These are creating major changes in the way that we experience the provision of health care today.

1. Overview of the earlier healthcare system

In the recent past, health insurance plans were largely "fee-for-service." That is, physicians provided their services, and the health insurance companies paid whatever fee the physicians charged. Patients could usually choose the doctors and specialists they wanted under this system. Gradually, however, patients were required to pay annual deductibles and then to copay a certain portion of their medical bill. These measures were designed to cut down the costs of care, for policy makers thought that patients would use the healthcare system less often if they had to pay toward their care. Less use, they believed, meant lower expenditures for health care. "Fee-for-service" plans also began to vary in their coverage of hospital care. Some covered the total cost of hospitalization; others required a separate hospital deductible. Yet the costs of health care continued to spiral and policy makers, insurance companies, and employers in the United States searched for additional ways to bring them under control.

2. Managed care and HMOs

Managed care was introduced in response to some of the high costs and inefficiencies of the older system of health care. It is based on the assumption that bringing health care into the marketplace as a commodity will decrease its costs, maintain its quality, and expand access to it. In a managed care system, the delivery of cost-effective health care is "managed" by administrators who try to ensure that money is not spent on inappropriate or unnecessary treatment, tests, and services. Expenses are also kept down by putting a ceiling on reimbursements to caregivers and by preventing patients from entering hospitals or other acute-care institutions when they can be treated less expensively at home, in outpatient settings, or in less costly facilities.

Many of us who have jobs purchase our health insurance through our employers. In recent years, when our insurance has come up for renewal we may have noticed that fewer "fee-for-service" plans have been offered to us. This is because insurers are moving away from a willingness to pay whatever healthcare costs are submitted to them and are moving toward systems that assure them in advance what the price of care will be. Employers, insurers, and public authorities now tend to pay a fixed fee for a particular package of services, not a fee for a particular service. If our employers have continued to provide "fee-for-service" insurance plans to us, our premiums for them are often significantly higher than under our old plans, and we have been limited to a list of preferred physician providers (PPOs). Some of us have found that our choice of a healthcare plan has been from among managed care programs only.

One of the primary ways in which to provide managed care is through health maintenance organizations (HMOs). These organizations offer patients an approved list of primary care physicians who act as "gatekeepers." Whether we can choose our primary physician from among them and whether we will see the same primary physician every time we need medical care varies with the particular HMO. We can see specialists, under the rules of most HMOs, if, in the professional judgment of our primary physician, we need more specialized care. Since we cannot go to any physician or hospital we choose but must go to a physician affiliated with our HMO, these organizations can keep down their expenses for physicians and healthcare facilities by making arrangements with them that are less costly than they would be otherwise. Moreover, HMOs cover large numbers of individuals and thus have market power, which means that they can drive a bargain to purchase medical services at a lower cost than would otherwise be possible.

3. Ways in which some managed care plans restrict services to save money

Until recently, managed care plans could refuse to accept individuals with a history of illness (known as a "preexisting condition") in order to keep their expenses down. This resulted in the loss of insurance for some with a preexisting condition who changed jobs or insurers. Concern about the health of these individuals led Congress to pass legislation protecting them from being denied insurance if they have been continually insured for at least the twelve previous months. This legislation, however, does not protect them from having to pay higher premiums.

Some managed care plans require individuals to pay part of the cost of services they receive in the hope that this will lead patients to use services less often. Some also limit the number of visits to a doctor or days of care in a healthcare facility that they will cover. Others set a limit on the dollar amount of the payments they allow for medical services during a defined period. These are all ways of limiting the services that individuals in an HMO receive, in an attempt to save money.

Managed care systems may also try to limit services by giving doctors certain incentives or penalties. Some plans offer financial incentives to doctors and institutions to provide less care than they might otherwise by establishing a fixed payment that they receive per day, per illness, or per person, regardless of how much treatment they actually provide. Others offer bonuses to physicians at the end of the year if costs are down. Doctors and healthcare institutions working in such systems end up with the same amount of money per patient, no matter how much or how little care they provide (except for "outliers," or patients whose care costs an extraordinary amount of money). They therefore are less apt to overtreat patients, administrators of managed care plans believe.

Many health plans insist that some services that doctors propose to provide to patients must be approved in advance. Certain decisions, such as those about hospital admissions and the use of certain medical procedures, must be approved by special HMO personnel known as "resource utilization managers." Some plans may establish "productivity standards," requiring doctors to treat a certain number of patients on average per day. In effect, this means that doctors must limit the time they spend with patients in discussing treatment options in order to meet these standards. Doctors who do not conform to preadmission review requirements or to productivity standards run the danger of being ousted from the HMO for which they work.

4. Advantages of managed care

Most of us approve of efforts to save money on the cost of medical care if this does not diminish the quality of that care. Managed care organizations encourage the economical use of healthcare services while attempting to maintain an appropriate level of care. Preliminary national standards to measure the quality of care are currently being developed in an effort to promote good quality care while keeping costs down.

Managed care tends to give greater attention to preventing illness than did traditional "fee-for-service" medicine. This is an advantage, for most patients would rather avoid an illness than experience it. Further, "managed care" can reduce the amount of unnecessary treatment those who fall ill receive. Moreover, through its use of healthcare teams, managed care plans maintain that they can allow greater continuity of care than under the old "fee-for-service" system. Patients, it is assumed, are at an advantage if they are followed by the same basic group of caregivers over the course of time they remain in the plan.

5. Disadvantages of managed care

Perhaps the greatest disadvantage of managed care is that patients are not guaranteed any voice in deciding what sort of care they think is best for them. They are, by and large, cut out of policy decisions that would allow their views of a good life and a good death to be heard and put into effect. The goals governing managed care organizations are determined by the corporation that owns them in light of what will provide the most efficient service at the lowest cost. Since there are no national standards of "quality" care, this is determined by those running HMOs and other managed care groups, and their need to make a profit for shareholders is bound to have an impact on their decisions. A just use of our healthcare resources requires limiting treatment that offers only marginal benefit at great cost, but managed care organizations present the danger that they may not offer care that offers substantial benefits at a reasonable cost.

Ironically, although the policies of managed care organizations were expected to cut costs, this has not necessarily occurred.

States that have required Medicaid patients to use managed care have been disappointed to see few savings. Moreover, some patients and doctors are concerned that this form of care may lead to underservice of those in need of treatment. Managed care plans are usually designed to care for relatively healthy people, and critics fear that those who are seriously or chronically ill will not receive care because they will not be admitted to an HMO.

Patients who belong to HMOs may find they have increased waiting times for appointments and that they must call ahead for permission to be seen in an emergency room. Rather than experiencing greater continuity of care, some find that discontinuity of care prevails. Which physicians treat them seems more a matter of chance than of team scheduling in response to patient need. Moreover, some HMO managers cut costs by limiting which medications physicians can prescribe, regulating how often physicians can see patients, determining when physicians can refer patients to specialists, and prescribing which procedures physicians can perform. Primary care physicians are providing more and more specialty care for which they may have no training, and specialists are being asked to treat routine problems of the entire body with which they may not be familiar.

Although some of these measures encourage doctors to provide good care more economically, some doctors believe that at times they impinge on medical practice in ways that result in an unacceptably low quality of care and in patient suffering. Critics cite the motto at one managed care plan, "Greet 'em, treat 'em, and street 'em," as illustrative of the goals they believe managed care promotes of hurrying patients through the system and undertreating them.

In some managed care systems, doctors feel pressured to follow these cost-cutting policies because they will lose their jobs if they refuse. The possibility of such loss is bound to shape the decisions caregivers make about patient care. Those who raise this concern say that when physicians are forced to choose between the good of their patients and their professional survival, the bond of trust between doctors and patients is bound to weaken. Health care, they declare, is a form of ministry. Physicians and nurses have an obligation of stewardship of their professional knowledge and are called to use it to heal patients and to comfort them when healing is not possible. When managed care plans pit the welfare of patients against the professional and even personal survival of caregivers, they wrongly introduce into treatment decisions factors that are extraneous to the good of the patient and the professional call of caregivers.

Some managed care organizations are attempting to respond to these issues and are providing forums in which doctors can express their concerns about policies they believe lead to undertreatment and an inadequate quality of care without fear of losing their employment. Some HMOs survey members and change those policies that members indicate are not promoting good care. Congress and state legislatures have also become involved in attempting to assure that managed care systems provide what they consider good quality care. However, it may be neither practical nor possible to legislate safe medical care procedure by procedure. Moreover, patients in need of care or denied care are not usually in a position to initiate a protest that will be heard by those administering managed care plans. As Pellegrino observes, ". . . a [grievance] process might be of use retrospectively to patients seeking retribution for harm done, but it is an unrealistic safeguard at the time the injustice is being perpetrated." The measures suggested above provide at least a starting point for reconsidering the ways in which we provide health care to our population.

6. Impact of managed care on insurance coverage of those sixty-five and older

Medicare provides significant health benefits for those of us who are sixty-five and over. Those who administer this program are also looking for ways to stem rising healthcare costs. They are attempting to do so by enrolling a larger number of recipients in managed care plans. Those of us on Medicare who decide to sign up with an HMO plan give the management and control of our basic Medicare benefits to the HMO, which then functions in the way described above. Our selection of physicians is limited to the HMO list of doctors who carry out the policies of the managing corporation. If we try an HMO and are not satisfied with it, we may find it difficult to return to the standard form of Medicare we once had. A 10 percent penalty on premiums may be involved on Medicare Part B, and we will probably have to wait for an open enrollment period to sign up for a new policy. Therefore, those of us who enroll in a Medicare HMO and decide to switch back to the older system should not drop the HMO until we are able to enroll in another Medicare plan.

Appendix C. Resolutions of the General Convention of the Episcopal Church Relating to Crucial Medical Treatment Decisions Near the End of Life

I. Advance directives

Approve the Use of a Living Will: Sixty-Seventh General Convention of 1982 [C002]

Resolved, the House of Bishops concurring, That the Episcopal Church recognize and approve the Living Will as a beneficial document to be used by individuals throughout the Church as a tool for discussing one's medical wishes before the time comes when one is not otherwise able to communicate these wishes.

(General Convention, *Journal of the General Convention of . . . The Episcopal Church, 1982* [New York: General Convention, 1983], p. C-147.)

Reaffirm the 1982 Resolution on the "Living Will": Seventieth General Convention of 1991

Resolved, the House of Bishops concurring, That the 70th General Convention reaffirms its 1982 resolution (1982-C002a) recognizing and approving the "Living Will" (Advance Directive) as a beneficial document to be used by individuals as a tool for discussing one's medical wishes before the time of illness and impending death, and encourages both physicians and their patients to more faithfully and honestly pursue such discussion and the execution of such living wills; and be it further

Resolved, That this General Convention urges physicians, nurses, families, patients, surrogates and legislative bodies where necessary, to show aggressive commitment to the concept of allowing peaceful death in a setting that enables the patient to maintain control and dignity, free from intrusion of unwanted and inappropriate technology and also from intolerable suffering because of under-use of available pain medication, including narcotic drugs; and be it further

Resolved, That the Standing Commission on Human Affairs and Health and other appropriate bodies within the Church be urged to continue to study the complex issues surrounding the quality of life and terminal care, and especially the rightness of refusing life-saving treatments and the inappropriate use of technology in prolonging the act of dying or indefinitely sustaining persons who are in a permanent vegetative state.

(General Convention, *Journal of the General Convention of . . . The Episcopal Church, 1991* [New York: General Convention, 1992], p. 386.)

2. Making crucial decisions

Request Report on the Question of the Right to Die: Sixty-Ninth General Convention [B009]

Resolved, the House of Bishops concurring, That the Joint Commission on Human Affairs and Health be requested to study and report on the questions and concerns surrounding the right to die.

(General Convention, *Journal of the General Convention of . . . The Episcopal Church, 1988* [New York: General Convention, 1989], p. 293.)

Establish Principles with regard to the Prolongation of Life: Seventieth General Convention

Resolved, the House of Bishops concurring, That this 70th General Convention set forth the following principles and guidelines with regard to the forgoing of life-sustaining treatment in the light of our understanding of the sacredness of human life:

1. Although human life is sacred, death is part of the earthly cycle of life. There is a "time to be born and a time to die" (Ecclesiastes 3:2). The resurrection of Jesus Christ trans-

forms death into a transition to eternal life: "For as by a man came death, by a man has come also the resurrection of the dead" (1 Corinthians 15:21).

2. Despite this hope, it is morally wrong and unacceptable to take a human life in order to relieve the suffering caused by incurable illness. This would include the intentional shortening of another person's life by the use of a lethal dose of medication or poison, the use of lethal weapons, homicidal acts, and other forms of active euthanasia.

3. However, there is no moral obligation to prolong the act of dying by extraordinary means and at all costs if such dying person is ill and has no reasonable expectation of recovery.

4. In those cases involving persons who are in a comatose state from which there is no reasonable expectation of recovery, subject to legal restraints, this Church's members are urged to seek the advice and counsel of members of the Church community, and where appropriate, its sacramental life, in contemplating the withholding or removing of life-sustaining systems, including hydration and nutrition.

5. We acknowledge that the withholding or removing of life-sustaining systems has a tragic dimension. The decision to withhold or withdraw life-sustaining treatment should ultimately rest with the patient, or with the patient's surrogate decision-makers in the case of a mentally incapacitated patient. We therefore express our deep conviction that any proposed legislation on the part of national or state governments regarding the so called "right to die" issues, (a) must take special care to see that the individual's rights are respected and that the responsibility of individuals to reach informed decisions in this matter is acknowledged and honored, and (b) must also provide expressly for the withholding or withdrawing of life-sustaining systems, where the decision to withhold or withdraw life-sustaining systems has been arrived at with proper safeguards against abuse.

6. We acknowledge that there are circumstances in which health care providers, in good conscience, may decline to act on request to terminate life-sustaining systems if they object

on moral or religious grounds. In such cases we endorse the idea of respecting the patient's right to self-determination by permitting such patient to be transferred to another facility or physician willing to honor the patient's request, provided that the patient can readily, comfortably, and safely be transferred. We encourage health care providers who make it a policy to decline involvement in the termination of life-sustaining systems to communicate their policy to patients or their surrogates at the earliest opportunity, preferably before the patients or their surrogates have engaged the services of such a health care provider.

7. Advance written directives (so-called "living wills," "declarations concerning medical treatment" and "durable powers of attorney setting forth medical declarations") that make [known] a person's wishes concerning the continuation or withholding or removing of life-sustaining systems should be encouraged, and this Church's members are encouraged to execute such advance written directives during good health and competence and that the execution of such advance written directives constitute loving and moral acts.

8. We urge the Council of Seminary Deans, the Christian Education departments of each diocese, and those in charge of programs of continuing education for clergy and all others responsible for education programs in this Church to consider seriously the inclusion of basic training in issues of prolongation of life and death with dignity in their curricula and programs.

(General Convention, *Journal of the General Convention of . . . The Episcopal Church, 1991* [New York: General Convention, 1992], p. 383.)

Amend General Convention Principles on the Prolongation of Life: Seventy-First General Convention [A056]

Resolved, the House of Bishops concurring, That the 71st General Convention amend point two of the eight-point principles and guidelines concerning prolongation of life set forth in Resolution A093a of the 70th General Convention, to read as follows:

2. Despite this hope, it is morally wrong and unacceptable to take a human life in order to relieve the suffering caused by incurable illness. This would include the intentional shortening of another person's life by the use of a lethal dose of medication or poison, the use of lethal weapons, homicidal acts, and other forms of active euthanasia. Palliative treatment to relieve the pain of persons with progressive incurable illnesses, even if done with the knowledge that a hastened death may result, is consistent with theological tenets regarding the sanctity of life.

(General Convention, *Journal of the General Convention of... The Episcopal Church, 1994* [New York: General Convention, 1995], pp. 289–90.)

Appointment of a Working Group on End of Life Issues:
Seventy-Second General Convention [C013s]

Resolved, the House of Bishops concurring, That the 72nd General Convention request the appropriate Interim Body, as determined by the Presiding Bishop and the President of the House of Deputies, appoint members to a working group representing a wide range of expertise and approaches to medicine, ethics and theology; to study the theological and ethical implications of end of life issues, including adequate palliative care, euthanasia, and assisted suicide, taking into consideration pertinent studies in the Christian moral perspective such as the Washington Report, previous resolutions of the General Convention; and recent Supreme Court decisions, and report to the 73rd General Convention.

(General Convention, *Journal of the General Convention of... The Episcopal Church, 1997* [New York: General Convention, 1998] p. 184.)

3. The healthcare system

Advocate for Appropriate Health Care for All Who Are Ill:
Sixty-Ninth General Convention [D108]

Resolved, the House of Deputies concurring, That this 69th General Convention direct the Presiding Bishop and the Executive

Council, in light of the strains upon the health care system exerted by the AIDS Epidemic, to direct the Washington D.C. office of the Episcopal Church in the United States of America to adopt a strategy to advocate for all persons suffering from illness by creating appropriate levels of cost-effective health care, for example, hospices and alternative health care facilities.

(General Convention, *Journal of the General Convention of . . . The Episcopal Church, 1988* [New York: General Convention, 1989], p. 693.)

Advocate Legislation for Comprehensive Health Care: Seventieth General Convention [A010]

Resolved, the House of Deputies concurring, That this 70th General Convention assert the right of all individuals to medically necessary health care, including long-term services; and be it further

Resolved, That the Episcopal Church be encouraged at all levels to advocate for legislation for comprehensive medical benefits to include diagnostic tests, primary and tertiary care for acute and chronic conditions, rehabilitation care, long-term care, mental health services, dental care and prescription drugs; special attention should be given to the needs of individuals with limited self-care capabilities; and be it further

Resolved, That the Washington Office of the Episcopal Church, the Public Policy Network, the Office of Social and Specialized Ministries, and other appropriate agencies at the Episcopal Church Center facilitate the implementation of this resolution at the federal level.

(General Convention, *Journal of the General Convention of the . . . Episcopal Church, 1991* [New York: General Convention, 1992], p. 764.)

Recommend Every Diocese to Address Health Issues: Seventieth General Convention [A094]

Resolved, the House of Bishops concurring, That the 70th General Convention recommend that every diocese review the reports of the Standing Commission on Health and other resources nationally and locally, with the intention of addressing the issues, establishing guidelines for healthy Christian living, informing our members, assisting the Church in voicing ethical insights in national debates on health matters, and sharing our concern and support with those working in the field of health care.

(General Convention, *Journal of the General Convention of the . . . Episcopal Church, 1991* [New York: General Convention, 1992], p. 251.)

Call for a System of Universal Access to Health Care:
Seventieth General Convention [A099]

Resolved, the House of Deputies concurring, That the 70th General Convention decries the inequitable health care delivery system of the United States of America and calls upon the President, the Congress, Governors and other leaders to devise a system of universal access for the people of our country.

(General Convention, *Journal of the General Convention of the . . . Episcopal Church, 1991* [New York: General Convention, 1992], p. 610.)

Adopt Principles on Access to Health Care:
Seventy-First General Convention [A057]

Resolved, the House of Bishops concurring, That this 71st General Convention of the Episcopal Church adopt the following four principles as the position of the Episcopal Church regarding health care:

> That universal access to quality, cost effective, health care services be considered necessary for everyone in the population.

> That "quality health care" be defined so as to include programs in preventive medicine, where wellness is the first priority.

> That "quality health care" include interdisciplinary and interprofessional components to insure the care of the whole person—physiological, spiritual, psychological, social.

> That "quality health care" include the balanced distribution of resources so that no region of the country is underserved.

(General Convention, *Journal of the General Convention of the . . . Episcopal Church, 1994* [New York: General Convention, 1995], p. 288.)

Appendix D. Resources for Those Near the End of Life and Those Close to Them

AIDS Resource Center
275 Seventh Ave., 12th Floor
New York, NY 10001
Phone: (212) 633-2500

Alzheimer's Association
919 North Michigan Ave., Suite 1000
Chicago, IL 60611-1676
Phone: (800) 272-3900
Internet: www.alz.org

American Association for Retired Persons
Legal Council for the Elderly
601 E St., N. W.
Washington, D.C. 20049
Phone: (202) 434-2170
Internet: www.aarp.org/programs/legal

American Pain Society
4700 W. Lake Ave.
Glenview, IL 60025
Phone: (847) 375-4715
Fax: (847) 375-4777
Internet: www.ampainsoc.org
Email: info@ampainsoc.org

CancerCare
1180 Avenue of the Americas, 2nd Floor
New York, NY 10036
Phone: (800) 813-4673 or (212) 221-3300
Internet: www.cancercare.org

Center to Improve the Care of the Dying
George Washington University
1001 22nd St., N. W., Suite 820
Washington, D.C. 20037
Phone: (202) 467-2222
Fax: (202) 467-2271

Internet: www.gwu.edu/~cicd
Email: cicd@gwis2.circ.gwu.edu

Choice in Dying
20 Varick St.
New York, NY 10014-4810
Phone: (212) 366-5540
Fax: (212) 366-5337
Internet: www.choices.ord

Commission on Aging with Dignity
Five Wishes Living Will
P.O. Box 1661
Tallahassee, FL 32302
Phone: (800) 562-1931
Internet: www.agingwithdignity.org

Eldercare Locator
Administration on Aging
303 Independence Ave., S. W.
Washington, D.C. 20201
Phone: (800) 677-1116
Fax: (202) 260-1012
Internet: www.ageinfor.org.elderloc

Hospice Association of America
519 C St., N. E.
Stanton Park
Washington, D.C. 20002-5809
Phone: (202) 546-4759

Hospice Education Institute
"Hospice Link"
Five Essex Square
P.O. Box 713
Essex, CT 06426-0713
Phone: (800) 331-1620 or (203) 767-1620
Internet: nysernet.org/bcic/numbers/hospice.html

National Academy of Elderlaw Attorneys
1604 North Country Club Rd.

Tucson, AZ 85716
Phone: (520) 881-4005
Fax: (520) 325-7925
Internet: www.naela.org

National Hospice Organization
1901 N. Moore St., Suite 901
Arlington, VA 22209
Phone: (800) 658-8898 or (703) 243-5900

Visiting Nurse Association of America
11 Beacon St., Suite 910
Boston, MA 02108
Phone: (800) 426-2547

Glossary

AIDS or Acquired Immunodeficiency Syndrome is the final stage of infection caused by a virus (HIV or Human Immunodeficiency Virus) that over months and years gradually destroys the immune system by attacking certain of the white cells.

Advance directive is an instruction from a competent person, in writing or verbal, regarding his or her choices about future medical treatment in the event the person becomes unable to make decisions at a later time. An advance directive may specify which treatments a person consents to or refuses, designate a surrogate decision maker, or both. (See Section 3. e.)

Alzheimer's disease is the most common form of dementia. It is a chronic brain disease that leads to progressive loss of brain function and eventual death.

Artificial nutrition and hydration is a way of supplying nutrients and water to a person by such means as nasogastric tubes, surgically implanted stomach tubes (gastrostomies), and intravenous infusions. (See Section 5. c.)

Best interests standard is a legal standard to guide surrogate decision making when the preferences of the patient are not known. On this standard, the surrogate makes medical treatment decisions from the point of view of a hypothetical reasonable person on the basis of socially shared criteria. (See Section 3. d.)

Book of Common Prayer, The originally referred to the official service book of the Church of England. In it, the Latin services of the medieval church were simplified and compiled into a convenient one-volume work. As the Anglican Communion has grown, so various member churches have provided their own edition of *The Book of Common Prayer.* As the core document of worship and liturgy of the church, *The*

Book of Common Prayer has an extensive role in formulating the belief of Episcopalians. The Prayer Book undergoes periodic revision. The current *Book of Common Prayer* of the Episcopal Church was authorized in 1979; its predecessor, in 1928.

Brain death is taken as a sign of death and so is used to declare death. It is used only when the traditional signs of death—permanent stopping of spontaneous breathing and heartbeat—cannot be employed because a person's breathing and heartbeat are maintained by a machine. In brain death, the whole brain has stopped functioning and there is no possibility that a person in this condition will return to life. The person who is "brain dead" is considered legally dead according to the laws of many states in the United States. (See Appendix A.)

Cardiac arrest is the sudden stopping of the heart, a heart attack. (See Section 5. b.)

Cardiopulmonary resuscitation is a range of technologies used to restore and maintain blood circulation and breathing in a person who has experienced cardiac and/or respiratory arrest. (See Section 5. b.)

Central nervous system refers to the brain and spinal cord.

Chronic obstructive pulmonary disease (COPD) (also known as chronic obstructive lung disease) refers to several diseases that involve chronic limitation of the flow of air into the lungs: emphysema, asthma, chronic bronchitis, and less common diseases such as cystic fibrosis. COPD is a major cause of respiratory failure in elderly persons.

Coma is a state that results from damage to the upper cortex of the brain and the brain stem that renders persons unconscious and unable to function in many ways. Those in a coma seem asleep and unaware of the world. They may respond to treatment and recover consciousness. In general, comatose persons who survive begin to awaken and recover gradually within two to four weeks. Those who do not recover enter persistent vegetative state (PVS).

CT (computed tomography) scan shows sections of body part being visualized. The images are monitored on a video screen during the exam, so that the radiologist has a view of the inside of the body part. X ray, in contrast, shows only an outline of the entire body part.

"Disproportionately burdensome" treatment (also known as "extraordinary" treatment) is treatment that would provide more burdens than benefits, as these are determined by the patient according to his or her values and goals. Such treatment is not morally required. (See Section 4. a.)

Do Not Resuscitate (DNR) order (also known as a "No Code" order) is a directive by a physician to withhold cardiopulmonary resuscitation in the event that a patient experiences cardiac or respiratory arrest. Such orders are to be entered with the agreement of the patient or surrogate.

Durable power of attorney for health care is a form of advance directive in which a person designates a surrogate for healthcare decision-making purposes. The directive can be used for a broad range of health decisions, not only the withholding or withdrawing of life-sustaining treatment. (See Section 3. e.)

Electroencephalogram is a neurologic diagnostic procedure in which the spontaneous electrical activity of the brain is recorded by placing pairs of electrodes on the scalp in certain locations. Abnormal patterns diagnose disease; the absence of activity indicates brain death. (See Appendix A.)

Ethics committee is an advisory group within a hospital or other healthcare institution whose role is to analyze ethical dilemmas and to advise and educate health caregivers, patients, and families regarding difficult treatment decisions.

"Extraordinary" treatment. See "disproportionately burdensome" treatment.

Gastrostomy is a feeding tube surgically inserted through the patient's abdomen into the stomach. (See Section 5. c.)

Hospice is a method of care that provides supportive medical, social, and spiritual services for dying persons and their families. Hospice services can be provided in the patient's home, a nursing home, a hospital, a special hospice facility, or a combination of these.

Intravenous feeding is nutritional support administered through a vein.

Intubation is the insertion of a tube into a body opening or organ.

Life-sustaining treatment includes medical devices, drugs, or procedures that can keep patients alive who would otherwise die within a foreseeable, though usually uncertain, time.

"Living will" is a form of advance directive in which a person gives directions regarding medical care in the event of a terminal illness and, in some cases, a persistent vegetative state (PVS). (See Section 3. e.)

Magnetic resonance imaging (MRI) is a complicated, noninvasive diagnostic procedure that involves radiological techniques performed on a body part while in a magnetic field. The imaging gives structural and biochemical information about soft tissue that allows differentiation between the normal and the abnormal.

Nasogastric tube is a feeding tube inserted through a patient's nose, down the esophagus, and into a patient's stomach. (See Section 5. c.)

"Ordinary" treatment. See "proportionately beneficial" treatment.

Palliative care is treatment that aims both to provide total care and to relieve pain and other distressing symptoms when a patient cannot be cured. It is not intended to prolong life. This form of care often includes personal support and counseling by a team of caregivers from various disciplines who have had special training in the evaluation and treatment of pain. (See Section 6. d.)

Persistent vegetative state (PVS) results from damage to the brain that renders a person unconscious and unable to function in many ways. Those in PVS appear to be awake and have a sleep-wake cycle, but they give no meaningful responses to their surroundings. Although their eyes open periodically and they occasionally "make faces," shed tears, or even laugh, these are reflex actions, not knowing responses. Persons in PVS do not meet the criteria for brain death. They have lost the higher cerebral powers of the brain, but their brain stem remains intact, preserving their breathing and reflexes. They can remain in this state indefinitely. The American Neurological Association Committee on Ethical Affairs maintains that PVS can be diagnosed in patients with "a high degree of certainty by well-defined criteria." Once PVS has been diagnosed firmly, recovery is rare. (See Appendix A.)

Pneumocystis pneumonia is an infection of the lungs caused by an organism in the environment that generally does not harm people. However, the severely impaired immune system of some persons with AIDS makes them unable to combat this organism and this serious and debilitating type of pneumonia can result.

"Proportionately beneficial" treatment (also known as "ordinary" treatment) is treatment that offers more benefits than burdens as these are determined by the patient in light of his or her values and goals. Such treatment is considered morally required. (See Section 4. a.)

Reconciliation is the consciousness of being at peace with God and our neighbors about sins or offenses we have committed. Among Anglicans the normal means of reconciliation are private personal confession to God with the intention of amending one's life and restoring a relationship with any persons we may have offended, remedying where possible any injury we have done to them, and forgiving injuries done to us. For persons who still cannot achieve a consciousness of being at peace with God through these two means, the Anglican Church recommends confession of sins to a priest. The Service of Reconciliation of a Penitent in *The Book of Common Prayer* provides a means to confess to a priest, who provides spiritual advice and assurance of God's forgiveness.

Rector is usually the senior clergy person in a financially self-supporting parish or congregation. When a parish is either not self-supporting or perhaps very small in membership, the clergy person in charge may be titled "vicar."

Resuscitation refers to procedures for restoring heart rhythm and maintaining blood flow and breathing following cardiac or respiratory arrest. (See Section 5. b.)

Sacraments are rites of the church, normally administered by clergy, that are, in the words of *The Book of Common Prayer*, "outward and visible signs of inward and spiritual grace, given by Christ as a sure and certain means by which we receive the grace." Traditionally, Anglicans have recognized only Baptism and the Eucharist as fully meeting this definition. Many Anglicans, however, speak of five additional rites—Confirmation, Ordination, Holy Matrimony, Reconciliation of a Penitent, and Unction of the Sick—as Sacraments, and all Anglicans consider these other rites to be means of grace. *The Book of Common Prayer* provides forms for all of these rites.

Sanctity of life refers to the belief that life has great value because it is God-given.

Stroke refers to a set of symptoms in which a person develops sudden neurologic impairment due either to a hemorrhage or thrombosis in the blood vessels of the brain.

Substituted judgment is a legal standard for surrogate decision making. According to this standard, the surrogate makes the decision on the basis of what is known about the patient's personal values and preferences. (See Section 3. d.)

Surrogate is a person whom we have designated to make health-care decisions for us when we are not competent to do so ourselves. (See Section 3. e. through h.)

Terminally ill means that death is expected for a person in the near future, based on the diagnosis of an illness that has a predictably fatal progression and that cannot be stopped. The meaning of "in the near future" has been uncertain, ranging from hours or months, to a year or more. It is frequently taken to mean that a person will live for no more than six months.

Trauma is a wound or injury that is generally inflicted upon a person suddenly but may also be psychological in nature if caused by a painful emotional experience. ■

Bibliography

American Pain Society Quality of Care Committee. "Quality Improvement Guidelines for the Treatment of Acute Pain and Cancer Pain." *Journal of the American Medical Association* 273(23) (1995):1874–80.

Beauchamp, Tom L., and James F. Childress. *Principles of Biomedical Ethics.* 4th ed. New York: Oxford, 1994.

Beauchamp, Tom L., and Robert M.Veatch, eds. *Ethical Issues in Death and Dying.* 2nd ed. Upper Saddle River, N. J.: Prentice-Hall, 1996.

Beker, J. Christiaan. *Suffering and Hope: The Biblical Vision and the Human Predicament.* 2nd ed. Grand Rapids, Mich.: William B. Eerdmans Publishers, 1994.

Billings, J. "Comfort Measures for the Terminally Ill: Is Dehydration Painful?" *Journal of the American Geriatric Society* 33 (1985):808–810.

Bouma, Hessel, III, Douglas Diekema, Edward Langerak, Theodore Rottman, and Allen Verhey. *Christian Faith, Health, and Medical Practice.* Grand Rapids, Mich: William B. Eerdmans Publishers, 1989.

Brown, David. *Choices: Ethics and the Christian.* Oxford: Blackwell, 1983.

Byock, Ira. *Dying Well: The Prospect for Growth at the End of Life.* New York: Riverhead, 1997.

Cahill, Lisa Sowle, "A 'Natural Law' Reconsideration of Euthanasia," in *On Moral Medicine: Theological Perspectives in Medical Ethics.* Edited by Stephen E. Lammers and Allen Verhey. Grand Rapids, Mich: William B. Eerdmans Publishers, 1987, pp. 445–453.

Choice in Dying, Q & A: Dying at Home. Choice in Dying, 200 Varick St., New York, N.Y. 10014.

Cohen, Cynthia B. *Casebook on the Termination of Life-Sustaining Treatment and the Care of the Dying.* Bloomington: Indiana University Press, 1987.

Committee on Medical Ethics of the Episcopal Diocese of Washington. *Assisted Suicide and Euthanasia: Christian Moral Perspectives "The Washington Report."* Harrisburg, Pa.: Morehouse Publishing, 1997.

Elmen, Paul, ed. *The Anglican Moral Choice.* (Harrisburg, Pa.: Morehouse Publishing, 1983).

Ferrell, B. A. "Pain Evaluation and Management in the Nursing Home." *Annals of Internal Medicine* 123(9) (1995):681–87.

Fischer, Kathleen. *Winter Grace: Spirituality and Aging.* Nashville: Upper Room Books, 1998.

General Synod Board for Social Responsibility. *On Dying Well: An Anglican Contribution to the Debate on Euthanasia.* Newport and London: Church Information Office, 1975.

Gillick, Muriel. *Choosing Medical Care in Old Age: What Kind, How Much, When to Stop.* Cambridge: Harvard University Press, 1994.

Gustafson, James M. *Ethics from a Theological Perspective,* Vol. 2. Chicago: University of Chicago Press, 1981.

Hart, Thomas N. *The Art of Christian Listening.* New York and Ramsey, N.J.: Paulist Press, 1980.

Heavlin, Marilyn Willett. *Roses in December: Finding Strength within Grief.* Nashville: Thomas Nelson, 1993.

Holst, Lawrence E., ed. *Hospital Ministry: The Role of the Chaplain Today.* New York: Crossroad, 1992.

James, John W., and Frank Cherry. *The Grief Recovery Handbook.* New York: Harper Collins, 1989.

Koenig, Barbara A., and J. Gates-Wiliams. "Understanding Cultural Differences in Caring for Dying Patients." *Western Journal of Medicine* 30(11) (1995):244–49.

Kubler-Ross, Elisabeth. *Living with Death and Dying.* New York: Macmillan, 1981.

Lammers, Stephen E., and Allen Verhey, eds. *On Moral Medicine: Theological Perspectives in Medical Ethics.* Grand Rapids, Mich: William B. Eerdmans Publishers, 1987.

Lewis, C. S. *A Grief Observed.* 14th ed. New York: Seabury Press, 1961.

Lewis, C. S. *The Problem of Pain.* New York: Macmillan, 1943.

Lynn, Joanne. *By No Extraordinary Means: The Choice to Forego Life-Sustaining Food and Water.* Bloomington: Indiana University Press, 1986.

Maugans, Todd A. "The SPIRITual History." *Archives of Family Medicine* 5 (1997):11–16.

Meier, Diane E., R. S. Morison, and Christine K. Cassell. "Improving Palliative Care." *Annals of Internal Medicine* 127 (1997):225–30.

National Academy of Sciences, Institute of Medicine, Division of Health Care Services, Committee on Care at the End of Life. *Approaching Death: Improving Care at the End of Life.* Washington, D.C.: National Academy Press, 1997.

Newark, Diocese of. *Report of the Task Force on Assisted Suicide to the 122nd Convention of the Episcopal Diocese of Newark.* January 27, 1996.

New York State Task Force on Life and the Law. *When Death Is Sought: Assisted Suicide and Euthanasia in the Medical Context.* May 1994 (New York State Task Force on Life and the Law, 5 Penn Plaza, New York, N.Y. 10001-1803).

Pellegrino, Edmund D. "Managed Care at the Bedside: How Do We Look in the Moral Mirror?" *Kennedy Institute of Ethics Journal 1997* 7 (4):325.

President's Commission for the Study of Ethical Problems in Medicine and Biomedical and Behavioral Research. *Deciding to Forego Life-Sustaining Treatment.* Washington, D.C.: U.S. Government Printing Office, 1983.

Price, Eugenia. *Getting through the Night: Finding Your Way after the Loss of a Loved One.* New York: Ballantine Books, 1983.

Ramsey, Paul. *The Patient as Person: Explorations in Medical Ethics.* New Haven: Yale University Press, 1970.

Sedgwick, Timothy, and Philip Turner, eds. *The Crisis in Moral Teaching in the Episcopal Church.* Harrisburg, Pa: Morehouse Publishing, 1992.

Smith, David H. *Health and Medicine in the Anglican Tradition.* New York: Crossroad, 1986.

Sulmasy, Daniel P. "Managed Care and Managed Death." *Archives of Internal Medicine* 155(2) (1995):133–36.

The SUPPORT Principal Investigators. "A Controlled Trial to Improve Care for Seriously Ill Hospitalized Patients." *Journal of the American Medical Association*, 274 (1995):1591–98.

Switzer, David K. *The Minister as Crisis Counselor.* Nashville: Abingdon Press, 1983.

Sykes, Stephen, and John Booty, eds. *The Study of Anglicanism.* London and Philadelphia: SPCK and Fortress, 1988.

Taylor, Jeremy. "Holy Living and Holy Dying," in *Jeremy Taylor: Selected Works.* Edited by Thomas K. Carroll. New York: Paulist Press, 1990, pp. 427–504.

Tournier, Paul. *A Listening Ear: Reflections on Christian Caring.* Minneapolis: Augsburg, 1987.

Veatch, Robert N. *Death, Dying, and the Biological Revolution.* Revised edition. New Haven: Yale University Press: 1989.

von Guten, C., K. Martinez, P. Neeley, and J. H. Von Roenn. "AIDS and Palliative Medicine: Medical Treatment Issues," *Journal of Palliative Care.* 11(2) (1995):55–59.

Washington, Episcopal Diocese of, Committee on Medical Ethics. *Before You Need Them: Advance Directives for Health Care, Living Wills and Durable Powers of Attorney.* Cincinnati: Forward Movement, 1995.

Wennberg, Robert N. *Terminal Choices: Euthanasia, Suicide, and the Right to Die.* Grand Rapids, Mich: William B. Eerdmans Publishers, 1989.

Wheeler, Sondra Ely. *Stewards of Life: Bioethics and Pastoral Care.* Nashville: Abingdon Press, 1996.

Wicks, Robert J., Richard D. Parsons, and Donald E. Capps, eds. *Clinical Handbook of Pastoral Counseling.* New York and Mahwah, N.J.: Paulist Press, 1985.

Williams, Philip. *When a Loved One Dies: Meditations for the Journey through Grief.* Minneapolis: Augsburg, 1995.

Wolf, Susan M., Cynthia B. Cohen, Bruce Jennings, Paul Homer, Daniel Callahan, and The Hastings Center Study Group. *Guidelines on the Termination of Life-Sustaining Treatment and the Care of the Dying.* Bloomington: Indiana University Press, 1987. ∎

Committee Members
Who Developed This Book

The following members of the Committee on Medical Ethics, Episcopal Diocese of Washington, [D.C], wrote, researched, edited, or otherwise assisted in developing this report.

The Reverend David Bird, Ph.D., Co-chair of the Committee on Medical Ethics of the Diocese of Washington, is rector of Grace Church, Georgetown, and co-editor of *Receiving the Vision: The Anglican-Roman Catholic Reality Today.* Previously, he served as canon theologian of the Diocese of Pittsburgh, was rector of St. Andrew's Church, New Kensington, Pennsylvania, and taught theology at Duquesne University.

Priscilla Cherouny, M. Div., is the mother of four grown children and the grandmother of two little granddaughters. She is a graduate of the Virginia Theological Seminary and has served on the staff of several parishes and as a chaplain in hospitals and nursing homes in the Washington metropolitan area. She currently ministers to four area nursing homes and is the pastoral assistant at St. James Episcopal Church in Potomac, Maryland.

Cynthia B. Cohen, Ph.D., J.D., Chair of the Committee on Medical Ethics of the Diocese of Washington, is a Senior Research Fellow at the Kennedy Institute of Ethics at Georgetown University and Adjunct Associate at The Hastings Center in New York. She has also chaired the Philosophy Department at the University of Denver, taught medical ethics at two medical schools, and served as associate to a hospital legal counsel. She has written and edited several books, including *Casebook on the Termination of Life-Sustaining Treatment and the Care of the Dying.*

Frank W. Cornett, M.D., J.D., is a physician and an attorney who currently practices medicine and works as a consultant in medical malpractice in Washington, D.C. He grew up in Nevada and attended college and medical school at the University of Nevada. He studied law at the University of California, Berkeley, and Harvard Law School. He first became interested in medical ethics, especially from a Christian and Anglican standpoint, while in college.

Alex Hagerty is married and has two children. He works as a manufacturer's representative. He is captain of the Arlington County Volunteer Fire Department, where he is a certified Emergency Medical Technician (EMT), a firefighter, and an emergency vehicle operator. He joined the Committee on Medical Ethics because of morally ambiguous situations he encountered as a volunteer fireman. Concern for what Do Not Resuscitate orders mean and what their effect is on rescue personnel brought him to the committee.

Patricia Lusk, M.P.H., R.N.C., L.N.H., is Director of Adult and Geriatric Health, Prince George's County Health Department, Maryland. As a registered nurse and director of a nursing home licensing program, she finds it impossible not to be concerned about the galloping advance of technology and the omission of ethical considerations in the current healthcare system and future health planning. She is hopeful that the work of the Committee on Medical Ethics of the Diocese of Washington will help to raise significant bioethical issues for public dialogue.

Virginia Oler, M.D., after finishing high school in Swarthmore, Pennsylvania, was graduated from the College for Women at the University of Pennsylvania in 1945. She was graduated from the School of Medicine in 1949, interned at the Hospital of the University of Pennsylvania, and served there as a Fellow in Gastroenterology. In 1952, she moved to Washington with her husband, Wesley M. Oler, M.D., an internist, and she worked for the D.C. Maternal Health and Child Welfare Service until she had her family. She has completed several bioethics courses at the Kennedy Institute of Ethics at Georgetown University and at Wesley Theological Seminary.

Dorothy Rainey is a layperson at St. John's Church, Lafayette Square, Washington, D.C., with a long-standing interest in bioethics issues. She has served on the vestry and many other committees of the church. World War II interrupted her college education at the University of Montana, where she was an English major. She married a career naval officer, raised a family, and, in the course of many moves, was always active in local Episcopal churches. She worked for several years at the Kennedy Institute of Ethics at Georgetown University in Washington, D.C., first as a volunteer, then as administrative assistant. She is currently the secretary of the Committee on Medical Ethics of the Diocese of Washington.

The Reverend George Timberlake, Th.M., is a chaplain at the U.S. Soldiers' and Airmen's Home, Washington, D.C. His primary work is in the long-term nursing facility where he serves on the Interdisciplinary Committee to plan care of residents. He has also been active in the Alcohol and Drug Abuse Program. He has served on the Bioethics Committee of the Home since its inception in 1987 and for the past two years has chaired that committee. Mr. Timberlake is a graduate of Kenyon College and Bexley Hall. He was ordained into the priesthood of the Episcopal Church in 1950. He received a Masters of Theology degree from Western Theological Seminary in 1969.

The Reverend Joseph Trigg, Ph.D., is the rector of Christ Church, Port Tobacco Parish, La Plata, Maryland, and teaches in an adjunct capacity at the Virginia Theological Seminary. He has also taught in the Early Christian Studies Department at the Catholic University of America. He earned a doctorate in the History of Christianity at the University of Chicago Divinity School, where his principal focus was on early Christian theology and ethics. He is the author of books on Origen and early biblical interpretation, as well as translations, articles, and reviews in academic and church-related publications.